THE *Art* OF
JOYFUL
LIVING

THE *Art* OF JOYFUL LIVING

SWAMI RAMA

HIMALAYAN INSTITUTE
PRESS

Honesdale, Pennsylvania, USA

Himalayan Institute Press
RR 1, Box 1129
Honesdale, Pennsylvania 18431-9706

© 1989, © 1996, © 2003 by The Himalayan International Institute
of Yoga Science and Philosophy of the U.S.A.

07 06 05 04 03   11 10 9 8 7
Seventh Printing

The paper used in this publication meets the minimum requirements
of American National Standard for Information Sciences—
Permanence of Paper for Printed Library Materials, ANSI
Z39.48-1984.

Library of Congress Cataloging-in-Publication Data
Rama, Swami, 1925-1996
  The art of joyful living / Swami Rama
    p. cm.
  Originally published: Honesdale, Pa.: Himalayan International
Institute of Yoga Science and Philosophy of the U.S.A., c1989
  ISBN 0-89389-236-X (alk.paper)
    1. Meditation. 2. Spiritual life. 3. Conduct of life. I. Title.

BL627.R336 2003
294.5'44--dc22   2003056837

CONTENTS

FOREWORD

The Art of Joyful Living is the testimony of someone who lived life in all its fullness. Its author, Swami Rama, assumed and renounced many large roles, both worldly and spiritual, marked by extremes and contrasts, in the course of his long lifetime. A brief glimpse of these events will help you understand how he mastered the art of joyful living and why he was uniquely qualified to teach this art to others.

Swami Rama was born to an aging Brahmin couple. Soon afterward, his father died, his mother lost her sight, and he was adopted by a Bengali saint. The boy grew up in the cave monasteries of the Himalayas but received a Western-style education, first at Woodstock (a secondary school in Mussourie), then at the University of Allahabad. After that, in an attempt to understand the mystery of life and the world in which he lived, he journeyed throughout the Indian subcontinent, living with accomplished masters and studying with great teachers such as Mahatma Gandhi and Rabindranath Tagore. At the age of twenty-four, he became Shankaracharya, the highest position in Hinduism. Three years later, he renounced this exalted post, got married, and had two children. Then he became a monk.

After twelve years of living in solitude, Swami Rama came to the West, where he founded the Himalayan Institute, a multi-national organization dedicated to teaching yoga, ayurveda, holistic health, and spirituality. As president of the Himalayan Institute, he worked both as a teacher and as an administrator. And even though he had a strong personal preference for solitude and was deeply committed to spiritual practice, he involved himself in the affairs of the world—traveling, lecturing, writing books, guiding students from all walks of life, managing the Institute's business. In other words, he was fully engaged with the complexities of modern life.

Even without knowing the details, you can see from this brief sketch that Swami Rama was extraordinary. But what cannot be so easily seen is that his life was also full of difficulties: the losses in early childhood, the transition from the cave monasteries to modern Western-style schools, the burden of Hinduism's most powerful office, and the end of his marriage. I came to know many of the details during the twenty years that I lived and studied with him, yet I found him unaffected by these difficulties. He was vibrant, energetic, and joyful. Even in his seventies, his eyes twinkled with the mischief of a child. He lived in the present and engaged in trivial, mundane activities with the same exuberant energy that he brought to profound spiritual matters.

When I expressed my puzzlement about how he had mastered the art of living so joyfully in both worlds—the profane and the sacred—he replied, "People are caught in their self-created misery. First they build a high, thick wall separating daily life from what they consider spiritual, then they exhaust themselves trying to demolish it. You are a creation of God, but happiness is your own creation. . . . Once you know the meaning and purpose of life, you will no longer waste your time grieving over the past and brooding about the future. You will see that life is a beautiful song and you will begin to enjoy its rhythm and melody. The creativity of the creator residing in you will begin to flow through you, spontaneously and effortlessly. Then you will no longer seek freedom from the world; you will experience freedom in the world."

Swami Rama's teachings can be summarized in one simple sentence: You can live a healthy and happy life, provided you understand that happiness is of your own creation. *The Art of Joyful Living* is a manual for learning how to be happy here and now. In the pages that follow, Swamiji discusses how to cultivate a calm and tranquil mind, how to turn it inward, and how to employ it to reflect on the meaning and higher purpose of life. Here you will learn that expectations are the source of misery, but that if you perform your duties selflessly and lovingly, you will remain free from all disappointment. The art of joyful living requires you to become the master of yourself—first, to master your own body and mind, and then, to masterfully transform the world around you. This book tells you how.

Pandit Rajmani Tigunait, Ph.D.
Spiritual Head, Himalayan Institute
August 2003

Chapter 1

KNOWING YOUR OWN TRUE SELF

You all want to know the reality that is eternal; you want to experience the state of peace and equilibrium that is your essential nature—the center of consciousness within. And yet your mind and personality prevent you from experiencing that finest level of yourself. In the ancient teachings it is said that time, space, and causation are the three prime conditionings or filters that affect the mind. But you can lead your mind beyond these conditions.

Time is the most powerful of all the "filters" that condition the mind. It is a powerful filter of reality. For example, perhaps you are sad today, but even so, a time comes when you laugh. Or perhaps you have been laughing and feeling good; still a time will come when you become sad. Thus, time affects your mind. Every state of mind is transitory and limited by time.

It is important to understand and recognize how time affects the mind, and you can better understand this by considering the nature of space. If you can fully understand how space is created, then time will no longer deter you; you will go beyond both time and space. For example, if I draw two lines, then there is space between the first line and the other. If there is no space, there is only one; then where is time?

Time and space exist only when there is a division, when you are divided within yourself. When you are one with yourself, then time, space, and causation—the three conditionings and limitations of the mind—are left behind and you go forward to a higher experience.

Since childhood you have all been listening in church and to your parents, who have told you that you should find God, but in fact, you already have him, because he is omnipresent. What you don't have, what you have not attained, is yourself. So the human endeavor and purpose is not actually to attain God. Your endeavor should really be to attain yourself. When you truly know yourself, when you realize yourself, then you will understand that you have also realized God. That which you call God today, you will understand fully when you know yourself on the deepest level.

I am not talking about knowing the mere self alone. There are actually two concepts of self: the first is the mere self and the second is the real self. The mere self is that self which changes over time, the self that has been conditioned, learned, and acquired. Nature changes, forms change, and even your name changes, but the real self never changes.

If the real self changed, then the very summum bonum of life would be changed, and then life itself would crumble. Everything that exists—all that can be seen, all that moves and changes this whole wheel of the universe—rotates on the foundation of that which does not move. If that unmoving something starts to move, then this external wheel of the universe will no longer rotate. The external frame of a wheel moves, yet the center hub of the wheel remains steady. If the hub moves, then the whole wheel will not rotate. In that same manner, there is something in you that moves; you are like a wheel in motion. But there is also something in you, a hub within you, that does not move—yet it moves with you wherever you go. You should try to understand this metaphor.

I am talking about that self which is the very cause of all your movements. Consider this a little more subtly: a wheel moves because of its spokes. Your hub is within and the external wheel is outside, and yet if there are no spokes the wheel will not move. You are not moving in the world because of your soul, the hub; you are moving because of the various faculties of the mind, which are the spokes. You cannot ignore their influence. Reality is your center hub, but to know that inner cause of all your movements, you first have to know the nature of these faculties which make you move.

There are three aspects of yourself to understand: that which moves, that through which it moves, and that which is the cause of the movement. You have to clearly understand these three aspects to fully understand yourself. The nature of the hub within cannot be imagined with the mind, because your mind is conditioned by time, space, and causation. Your human effort is to know your entire self—the self that moves, the subtler self that motivates us to move, and the subtlest self that is the cause of movement. That is why you should distinguish between the mere self and the real self.

We will explore the mere self first. Perhaps your mother gave you a particular name and told you that you were far superior to other children. Then you took that idea into your mind, although you never tried to understand it, and now you act according to that idea of your superiority. That is your mere self, the sense of self you acquired. When you are involved in that mere self so deeply, you are strengthening and feeding your ego again and again, and because of that your development does not go beyond that ego or limited sense of self.

That which separates you from your real self, the whole and real self, is your ego. You may wonder how you can cut down that ego, or you may try to tear it down or forget it, but that's not possible. Instead, you have to learn to "polish" or train your ego. When the ego becomes aware of the reality, it is trained, and then the ego is useful. If the ego does not remain aware of the reality, then the ego is not helpful; it is then harmful, or an obstacle.

The mind is a great tool that you can learn to use when you know about its various faculties, or functions. The mind has four main faculties. The first is *ahamkara*, or ego. That which says, "This is mine, this is me," is ego. When you become dishonest with yourself you become egotistical, and whenever you are egotistical, you are also dishonest with yourself. The more egotistical you are, the more dishonest you are, and then your dishonesty is also reflected to others. *Buddhi*, the faculty of intellect, is the function of mind that knows, decides, and judges. *Manas* is the faculty that produces data for you from the external world. It is also the faculty that doubts and questions. The final function of mind is *chitta*, the reservoir of impressions and memories. Learning how to coordinate these four functions of mind will be discussed in a later chapter. For now, it is important only to understand that they are not the real self.

If you want to know your true self, you should understand that it is neither your mind nor your personality. The personality is something outside your true self. The word "personality" comes from its root word, *persona*, a Greek word that refers to masks. If you remove all the coverings and veils of your personality, one by one, you will find the real light within. You will find the real self. In meditation you learn to go inside to this source and this light. You are not searching for something outside yourself. You are searching for someone who is already within you, so it is actually easy to find. But, unfortunately, since your childhood you have not been trained to see things in the internal world; instead, you have been taught to see things and to watch and judge things in the external world. No one teaches you how to look within, to find something within, to go to the source within. This subtle teaching is missing in your home life.

In other times, something unique took place. In India, for example, the mother-in-law had a great responsibility in the family's education. As soon as her daughter-in-law came to her home, the mother-in-law would take her outside and say, "Do you see that star?"

And the daughter-in-law would reply, "Oh, yes, everyone sees that."

And the mother-in-law would continue, "Do you see the star next to it?"

For a moment the daughter-in-law would be quiet, and then she would reply, "Now I can see it."

And the mother-in-law would continue, "Yes, it is also possible to see that, but do you see still another star next to that?"

And the daughter-in-law would answer, "No."

The mother-in-law would then say, "My duty is to help you to see that."

My duty as a teacher is to show you how to see that which is subtle, that which is not easily seen, to understand not only the external wheel and these various functions of mind, but to see and know the source within. The day that you see that face-to-face, you have accomplished your work as a human being—that is your human endeavor.

You need not become or attain God, and even if you could, you'd be sorry because if that happened you would no longer be understood by anybody. Strive instead for one goal: to understand your true self; learn how to know the self within. If you do not know yourself and you are trying to know God, it is not possible to do so.

Sometimes people shut out the idea of knowing themselves. They throw it away, and instead they have blind faith. But if you do this, your faith will waiver because it is not reasoned faith. It has not been assimilated by the mind. Your mind will always come between you and your faith. Such faith will not fully develop because your mind will not allow you to maintain it.

As a child I was very close to my master, so I had a special privilege. He was very loving to all, but he had a special love for me, and I was very possessive of him. One day I got angry with him. I said, "After all these years you still have not shown me God. All these great swamis come to you to learn and they go away happily, saying that they have attained something, but I have not attained anything. I don't want to be a hypocrite any more. Show me God, or I will leave you in the morning!" I was really a brat!

When I said that to him, he said, "Tomorrow morning I will show you God." I was so excited that I couldn't eat my supper; I was so excited that I was not really all there. I said to myself, "He doesn't lie, and if he said he'd do it, then he will."

I asked him, "Can you tell me one thing: why didn't you show me God seventeen years ago? Why are you doing it now, after all these years?"

He replied, "You never asked to see God before. Today you asked me, so I will definitely show you God in the morning."

I was so restless I could barely sleep the whole night. I said, "O Lord, let the sun rise and shine so that this morning I can go to my master and he can show me God!"

When the morning came, I woke. In those days, I took my bath early in the morning in the Ganges, even in winter, but that day I didn't feel the cold water. I took my bath and went to stand in front of him—excited, emotional, and completely wrecked and disorganized in my mind. I was extraordinarily devoted to him that morning; I prostrated and bowed to him. When you live with somebody you don't observe such formalities every day. Usually, I'd say simply, "Good morning,

Sir," because I was there all the time, but that day I brought him some wildflowers, and he gave me a look and said, "What is this abnormal behavior?"

I said, "You are going to show me God."

He said, "That is why you are doing all these rituals? Okay, son, sit down. First, tell me what type of God you want to see."

I said, "Type of God? I never thought about that question! Are there types of God?"

He said, "Not really, but you must have your own concept of God, and I don't want to change your concept. Think about it, and however you conceive of God in your mind, whatever picture you have in your mind about God, I will show you God according to that concept."

I said, "But I have not yet formed any concept of God."

Then he replied, "The day you develop one, I'll show it to you."

His point was that it is our minds that create concepts like God. But the mind can never have a full concept of God, because the mind does not have such a vast capacity. God cannot be truly conceptualized by the human mind. Most of us create a limited concept of God and guru, and later on, we find that both are actually different from what we conceived.

In my case, for seventeen years I had had a notion of God which crumbled in five minutes' time. My master said, "Shall I show you God as it is, or do you want to see God the way you want to see him? If I show you God as it is, you will not believe it because the picture of it in your mind is different, and if I show you God the way you *think* it is, that image is already there. Either way, you will not be convinced. The best way is to understand yourself first."

As you go on increasing your understanding of yourself, you will find that your needs change. Today, you think you need to have a good home, or you think you need a good car or a good woman or a good man, but that too changes. Your necessities change in the process of your evolution. As you go on changing, your concepts will also change. So don't hanker after God; know about yourself first. You are fully equipped to know yourself; you have all the means and tools to do so. You do not have to run around for this. You cannot honestly say, "I am not capable of knowing myself."

You have grown up and you have seen the external world. Now you have to go through an internal process. I'm not saying that the external world should be ignored; instead, the external world should be arranged and managed in such a way that it does not create obstacles for you. But the external world cannot really help you know the internal self. Even if you use the largest telescope in the world to see the sun, moon, stars, and the entire galaxy, if you turn that telescope toward yourself, you will not see anything. Nothing external is going to help you in your quest. To see that inner self, you will have to use that light that is there even when there is no light existing outside you. That is the light, knowledge, and wisdom that tells you that you exist. You have to use that light as your guide, and you need to use a particular method to do this.

If your goal is to reach the end of the earth in the East and you spend your whole life walking, but you are walking in the other direction, you will only end up in the West. At present you are already walking, but you are walking in the wrong direction. Your efforts should be applied in a methodical manner and then they will help you. That particular method was systematized, organized, and codified long ago by a great man named Patanjali. He systematized the method of yoga.

There have been many scholarly commentaries on Patanjali's *Yoga Sutra* but they all miss something very practical. Such commentaries can only satisfy the intellect; they do not actually help you beyond that. The second sutra, *Yogash chitta vritti nirodha*, means "yoga is the control of the modifications of the mind." Patanjali said that yoga means having control of the mind's operations, or thought-waves. Many translators and commentators on the *Yoga Sutra* could not find a completely suitable English word for *nirodha*, so they used the verb "control." But this should not be understood to mean suppression. Control means "channeling," or "regulating." You use this word every day, just as you use many words, without knowing exactly what they mean, and this results in confusion.

Once, when Christ was speaking by the Sea of Galilee, his disciples begged him, "Master, don't speak to us in parables, because we don't understand what you are saying." Christ was on a different level spiritually than they were, and they did not understand his language. The same is true in your personal life—most of your arguments at home or elsewhere are because you do not understand each other's language. That is why you fight. If you do not communicate well with your husband, even though he is a good man and you are a good woman, it is because you don't understand each other's language. Sometimes, you are on one wavelength and your husband is on a different wavelength and you don't understand each other, although you both mean well.

To communicate with others you have to learn to communicate first with yourself. Your external communication begins on the thought level, not through your speech or action. All your problems can be solved if you understand this point. Your communication can be bad communication or good communication; it can be frustrating or pleasant—but communication always starts on the mental level. So work with your own mind and your mental communication first.

The various faculties of mind have different dominant qualities, and they work together, just as all your fingers work together. If one of your fingers is missing it is difficult to do certain things; if two of them are missing, it is even harder. By the same token, without mental understanding and coordination nothing in your life can function well. Sometimes, even though you are brilliant and your intellect (buddhi) is wonderful, either your ego or your manas does not allow buddhi to function smoothly. You need to learn how to coordinate these different faculties so that they work together harmoniously. In Western music, the term "harmony" refers to a way in which different notes are applied to complement each other, thus creating the harmony. The process you need to understand is how to allow your different mental faculties to work together to create harmony.

The external world is entirely different from the internal world. To know the internal world, you have to understand yourself systematically. In the West, everything external has been systematized, but nothing internal has been systematized. In the East, everything internal has been systematized, and now they are trying to create external systems that function well. In the West, you need to balance your lives. Just as you arrange things in a neat and orderly way in the external world, you can also arrange things in the internal world so that the mind functions well, the buddhi functions well, the ego functions well, and there is coordination and harmony within.

Instead, there are constant conflicts in your mind, and because they are not resolved you are always emotional. Your emotional life and those unresolved problems within constantly create conflicts for you. Those conflicts come out in anger and many other ways. And as long as there are conflicts in your mind, it means that you have not resolved certain things. Such conflicts create misery, and then you experience that misery. But you can resolve your conflicts yourself. No one else is going to resolve them for you.

In the external world, you may not really be happy, but when someone says, "How are you?" you say, "Fine!" and you make a certain gesture with your face. Your parents taught you to smile to be polite whether there is a reason to smile or not.

When I first visited New York, I had a problem because of this pattern. I was crossing the street and everyone was making this strange facial gesture at me. I wondered if something was wrong with my clothes, so I went back to my hotel room and put on another suit. But again, when I went out the door, someone made that expression at me. This happened many times, so finally, I stopped a man on the street and said, "Why are you making this face at me?"

He said, "Sir, I was smiling at you."

I said, "But that is not smiling!"

Such social behavior has become your nature. You make that gesture with your face, and then you become serious again. Everyone expects you to learn this. But such smiles are only momentary. They do not reflect your real feelings. They are all an act; you are hiding yourself and creating conflicts within.

Sometimes one part of your mind says you do not want to work today, but your intellect tells you that if you do not go to work, you will not get paid, and you will not be able to pay your bills. So you are going to work against your mind and your own attitudes. On the other hand, many times you go with one part of your mind and don't follow your intellect. So there is a constant division within you. That constant division creates a conflict, and such conflict within and without is the source of all disease, physical and emotional. Nobody outside yourself creates illness for you. Disease is constantly increasing, and the number of hospitals is increasing. Everybody is a patient. This is happening all over the world. Perhaps with one problem, you can be helped by a therapist. But if you have formed a bad habit of developing many problems again and again, no therapist can ever help you. Your best therapy is to learn to understand self-therapy, which begins when you first learn to communicate within yourself. It is your ignorance of your physical and mental habits that makes you sick.

When you are your own best friend, then you are the friend of all. As long as you are your own enemy, don't expect the world to be your friend. Then everyone seems to be bad, and everyone seems to be looking at you in a suspicious way—because that's what you think about yourself. The day you approve of yourself and fully accept yourself, on that same day the world will finally accept you. Just as your face is an index of your heart, your heart is an index of your soul. The way you feel and the way you think is the way that you act. You can help yourself.

The greatest disease of all is not heart disease, stroke, cancer, or any other physical disease. The greatest human disease is not fear; it is loneliness. In the modern world you have all the comforts of life and you are still lonely. You have a spouse—you live under the same roof, you share the same bed—and you are still lonely. You have all experienced it. That loneliness is deep within you; it is related to the deepest level of yourself and not to external things.

Once, many years ago, a prince went to see my master at his cave retreat. (The caves in the Himalayas were not holes; they were large monasteries.) I was young then, and when I was young I was very active, so I stood outside the cave. It was ten o'clock in the morning, and the prince came with all his secretaries and guards. He said, "Brahmachari, I want to see your master!"

I said, "Get out of this place! You cannot see my master!"

He told me I was very arrogant and irresponsible, and I said to him, "You are the one who is arrogant and irresponsible, not me!"

He realized that could be true, so then he said mildly, "Sir, can I please see your master?"

I said, "Now you can, because you are humble."

So he went inside and sat quietly. He said, "Good morning to you, sir." Because he was educated at Oxford

University, he could not say anything more meaningful. How is someone relating to you by saying "good morning" to you? These are Western mantras—you say "sorry," "good morning," and "good afternoon"—but they are merely external rituals.

My master merely nodded his head. The prince said, "Aren't you lonely, sir?"

My master said, "Yes, because you have come."

The prince did not understand what he meant, so my master said, "I was enjoying the company of my great friend within, and now you have come and made me lonely."

You are lonely because you have not attained or established real spirituality—that is why you are lonely. Consider who makes you lonely. The one you love or the one who claims to love you will make you lonely. Wanting to be in the company of someone to whom you are attached will make you lonely. You do not feel lonely because of outsiders or foreigners. It is the owners of your so-called love that make you lonely, because your love is not always constant. And this creates conflict.

But there is someone within you who is always the same, always constant, opening his arms to embrace you—the greatest friend you have. When everything in life becomes hazy, who is going to help you? No one can communicate with you at that time. You cannot speak to your wife or husband or friends even though they are prepared to help you. Your neighbor, your boss, everyone is prepared to help you, but you cannot speak to them. Only your own friend within will say, "I am here. Why are you troubled?" To establish this friendship, you have to be aware of that friend, to be aware that you have a friend within. Then, if you have established this friendship within, you are never lonely.

There is a parable in the Upanishads in which someone asks, "How do you see? Is it because of the sunlight? When there is no sunlight, is it because of the moonlight? When there is no moonlight, then is it fire that allows you to see? When there is no fire, then what helps you see?" Even in the deepest darkness, you can see yourself. You don't see yourself through your eyes, yet you know you exist. I am talking about that which you don't see with your eyes, yet you know is right. You don't need any proof that you exist; you don't ask people, "Am I standing here?" You know it; you are here. You don't need any evidence of that.

A time will come when you will know your true self. You don't need a swami, a book, or a neighbor to tell you, "Yes, you are enlightened." To become enlightened is the human endeavor; don't stop pursuing that goal. The question is, how can this human endeavor be attained? First, you have to eliminate your foolish ideas, because otherwise they'll create a conflict in your mind. Without knowing yourself, you seek to know God; instead, seek to know yourself, and then you will easily know God. Your prime duty is to know yourself, and when you know the self of all, that is God.

How can you know this self? Through contemplation you can first know that your body is not the real self. Then you can eliminate your senses, your *prana*, your ego, and then your mind, because they all change. What is left is the true self. To understand the relationship between the true self and these superficial levels, imagine a light filtered by many shades. If you throw away all those filters, one by one, you will find the light inside. From a practical viewpoint, you can see light because of the real light that is already within you. You recognize the light of a light bulb, the light of the sun, the light of the moon, and the light of fire, because you have a light within. With the help of that light, you understand all the other lights. Yet you normally ignore your own light and search for the sunlight outside. Know your own light. This will help you to know and see all the other lights.

Chapter 2

POSITIVE LIVING AND THE
TRANSFORMATION OF HABIT PATTERNS

In the East, when we meet each other, we bring our hands together in a gesture of greeting and respect. This reminds us that the individual soul meets the cosmic soul, and we acknowledge the reality, "Thou art That." The gesture symbolizes the place where the two souls meet. But there's another reason why we bring our hands together—to remind us that the internal and external worlds must be brought into balance in order to fulfill the purpose of life.

The knowledge I have received is from the great sages and their sayings. But I have discovered that all over the world, both in the East and the West, people are not aware of the internal world because they have not yet understood themselves; they try, instead, to understand others. They analyze others without first understanding themselves and become judgmental. Whatever trait they dislike, they project it onto others, and then they say, "This person is like that." This habit of projection limits your growth throughout life, because as long as you project onto others you do not see yourself clearly.

Actually, there should be a smile on your face all the time, but to achieve that you need to have a clear concept of the meaning of life. You should understand something about the deeper philosophy of life. It is actually a simple philosophy, and once you understand it and are familiar with it, then you will start functioning on a different and deeper level. You will begin to enjoy your life. This does not mean enjoying something momentarily. Regardless of all that you have or don't have, within and without, you can enjoy life fully if you have the right philosophy.

Life is a manuscript, and the author of that manuscript is that which you are. Life is not a book written by someone else; you are the author of the manuscript that you are. That's life. The beginning and the ending of this manuscript are missing. You do not consciously know from where you have come, and you do not know where you will go. But you have the middle portion of the manuscript with you, and if you do not study that middle portion of the manuscript, which you are now, you will never search for and retrieve the missing pages.

Studying books can give you some solace in life, but I don't listen much to those who merely study books. I say, "If you study books all the time, when do you practice and when do you think?" and they have no answer for me. You should learn to study the greatest of all books, and that is the manuscript of your life. You are the creator of your own destiny. No one else creates problems, miseries or pains for you, not even God. God is the center of equality and love, so why should God be partial? Why should God make one person happy and another unhappy? That doesn't make any sense; whatever human beings experience, they think it is the result of God's will, but God does not make anyone unhappy. Happiness or unhappiness is of your own creation. To live is a gift, but to live happily is of your own making.

So you need to understand how you function; you need to understand the process that results in your actions. There is an important difference between an animal and a human being—your actions are very different from the actions of animals. In the animal kingdom we can observe that the activities of animals are basically controlled and governed by nature. But human beings are not totally governed by nature. You have a brain, you have a mind, and you have many faculties of mind such as buddhi, or intelligence. Your wisdom tells you that if it's raining, you can wear a coat, or use an umbrella, or make a shelter.

The human being is the finest of all species; there is no creature known so far that is higher than human beings. (Even *devas*, which are called "bright beings," or angels, aspire to be human beings.) You are the way you are because you wanted to be the way you are. And you can become the way you want to be. Don't postpone your improvement and enlightenment by saying, "Well, whatever God has created, I accept it." That is merely inertia or laziness—which is a sin. I don't really believe in such a thing as sin; sin merely means inertia. Sin means only that you're constantly hurting or harming yourself, or that you're not improving yourself. It means that you're not exploring the deeper dimensions of your life, or understanding your internal states. Sin means you are not evolving or attaining the next step of life. Throughout your life you have done experiments on matter, mind, and energy, but you have not done enough experiments on the real self within you; you've merely been repeating the word "God." And so just as your ancestors died, you will also leave your body. Nothing new or different is going to happen unless you work with yourself.

What good are the objects that you attain in the external world if you do not explore the inner dimensions of life? You do not need the happiness that comes for a moment and then makes you unhappy for minutes or hours. Happiness is that which is everlasting. Happiness is that which elevates you, that which you can share with others. You have formed a bad habit of sharing your grief and sorrows with others, but you do not share real happiness because you do not know what that is. No one has taught you how to look within, see within, and discover within. I am telling you to face this reality: the path to unfoldment and enlightenment is not austere, abstruse, or difficult. It's actually easy, and the easiest way to progress is to accept and understand yourself on all levels. To know yourself you don't need external crutches; you don't need gurus or teachers. Once you know the way, once you become aware of the goal and have determination, then it's easy for you to understand yourself.

The first real step is not to talk about knowing God, but to know yourself. So far, you have learned about yourself mainly through your body. You are a physical being, but knowing this level is not enough. You are also a breathing being, a sensing being, and a thinking being. All this takes place because you are that center of consciousness within, from where consciousness flows in various degrees and grades. On the journey within you explore who you are so that you can function well in your life, understand your habit patterns, and learn to live happily in the world. To learn that, you need to study yourself on three levels: action, speech, and mind. Any discipline you learn is meant to help you improve in these three dimensions.

The *Bhagavad Gita*, one of the major texts of India, contains the essence of the Vedas and Upanishads; it describes the importance of human actions when it says: "O human being, you can attain perfection by doing your own actions skillfully." This is a universal law: "As you sow, so shall you reap"—whatever actions you perform, they have their consequences. There is no "forgiveness" in this law; it is simply a matter of cause and effect. If you sow an apple seed, the tree will not give you pears. No matter how many times you pray for pears, that's not going to happen. Your prayers are a waste of time and energy because it is your actions that determine what you experience.

"Our childhoods are gone," you say, "and they will not return in this lifetime; is there any way that we can still improve ourselves?" The answer is that you can definitely improve and grow once you become aware of the fact that you are fully responsible for your actions. First, you must learn to act skillfully. Whatever action you perform, do so because you have assumed that action as your duty. Action has no meaning if it is not performed as a part of your duty. It becomes a part of your duty because you have assumed it as a duty and accepted it as such. So you must understand that when you perform an action, you are bound to reap its fruits. The fruits of those actions will then again motivate you to perform more actions, and from morning until evening, endlessly, throughout your whole life, you continue to act. There is no end to this process of action and reaction—it becomes a whirlpool for you.

How can you get out of this whirlpool? You cannot live without performing actions. Human beings must perform certain actions simply because they are human beings. This is the way your habits are formed: one day you perform a particular action, and the next day your memory of that experience leads you to perform that action again—and then again. And the more you repeat something, the deeper the groove it creates in your mind. That eventually becomes a habit.

Perhaps you think, "Oh, my habit is only superficial. I can stop drinking anytime," because you have not been drinking alcohol for a long time. On the other hand, sometimes when you examine a habit you realize, "I've been drinking for a long time; it's very difficult for me to stop now." Even so, you can change your behavior; you can definitely free yourself from the bondage of such addictions if you decide, "I need help," and firmly resolve to get it. There are people in the world who can help you if you really want help. Your problem is not a sin; it's only a bad habit.

If you examine yourself closely you will realize that your habits are your personality; they have created your personality. Your personality has been woven by your habit patterns, and your habit patterns are the result of your repetitive actions. No action can ever be performed unless you think or want it on some level of the mind, so your habits and personality are a reflection of that level. For example, if you don't even think of going in a certain direction, you will never end up there. The real motivation for each action is your thought. Before you express your thoughts and feelings, your habit patterns lead your mind to particular grooves, and then those grooves come forward and express themselves.

Your habits have a powerful role in your life and a strong influence on your spiritual development, and once you understand how to form habit patterns, you can understand the path of positive living. So learn to understand your habit patterns. Anything you do repeatedly creates a subtle groove in your unconscious mind, and then you don't have control over it any longer. Only by consciously creating a new groove will your mind begin to flow toward that new groove and you will form new habit patterns. The day you become aware that you are the master of your actions will be a great day for you; before you are aware of this, you are merely a slave to your own mind.

How do you tell which habit patterns are bad and which are good? Negative habit patterns are those that are injurious to your health on all levels—physical, mental, and spiritual. Good habit patterns are healthy and helpful to you. The Upanishads talk about *preyas* and *shreyas*. *Preyas* means "that which is pleasant"; *shreyas* means "that which is helpful." Sometimes that which is pleasant is not at all helpful to you; sometimes that which is helpful is not at all pleasant to you, especially at first, because of your negative habit patterns. So you have to understand what is really good for you, what is truly helpful for you. If I tell someone, "Please don't eat sugar," or, "Please don't be cross to your husband," that person may reply, "I love him, but what can I do, I'm just cross," or, "I can't stop eating sugar." The person knows that her husband is a wonderful man and she loves him very much, but when she eats sugar, it agitates her system and then she becomes cross and harsh with him.

This is a habit. You know that you are hurting yourself through such behavior, so don't look for a cause outside yourself. Nothing is going to help you if you do not decide to help yourself. But when you determine to improve, then Providence also helps you. If you help yourself to be sick, Providence will allow you to do that. When you repeatedly do something, it becomes an addiction. You know that the behavior is bad, yet you continue to do it. Nothing has clouded your power of knowing or your knowledge. But if you help yourself to be healthy, then Providence says, "I will supply all that you need to recharge your battery." You have to learn to practice and apply what you know.

For example, there was once a swami who used to teach every day. One of the students listened attentively and heard the swami speaking about *vairagya*, the philosophy of non-attachment. He took off for a forest dwelling, and after twelve years he was enlightened. He wondered what had been the fate of his friends, with whom he used to learn. So he returned to the ashram, and everyone was still sitting there exactly as before, and the swami was still teaching the same things.

What a waste of time! The point is that you don't need much external information; you already have true knowledge within. You need to learn how to apply the knowledge that you have. You are taught: "Be good, be nice, be gentle, be loving." You have all been taught that, but you should learn to practice, understand, and apply that knowledge to yourself.

These days human beings have all the imaginable comforts, but they are still not happy. They have no anchor in life; they have nothing to hold on to and are full of fear and misery. They are all so serious and no one seems to know how to truly smile. That is why I suggest that you meditate. Learn to be quiet for a few minutes every day so that the knowledge from the infinite library within you can come forward and make you aware that the purpose of life is not merely to earn a living. That is meant only to make you comfortable and secure so that you can attain the highest purpose of life. One part of your task is already over; you have attained the external means, but beyond that, you have not yet attained anything.

Try to work with yourself. Correct practice will lead you to perfection, so work with yourself. If you talk too much, for example, then decide that you will continue to speak and do so purposefully, but not uselessly. Those who speak too much usually speak nonsense. They don't say what they really want to say. You waste your energy through your speech, and this is also the case with your actions—you waste your energy by performing actions that are injurious for your health and your future. You should never give up working with yourself. It will weaken your willpower, and that is very destructive. Your willpower says, "I can do it; I will do it; I have to do it!" This is what you should always remind yourself: "I can do it; I will do it; and I have to do it!" If you fail and stumble once, try again. Don't give up. Giving up is defeat, and that defeat will cripple your inner sensitivity—and then you will lose that sensitivity.

So learn to discriminate. You don't need to make any external change to improve your inner situation; be wherever you are. Learn to decide things and to create determination, and you can attain the highest state. You'll never become lost if you search within, but you'll always be lost if you are searching for something outside yourself. The search lies within, from the gross self to the subtlest aspect of your being.

If you observe yourself, you will notice that you are negative much of the time. For example, a wife may worry because her husband has not come home on time. Perhaps he usually comes home at nine o'clock, and now it's already ten-thirty and he has not come back yet. If she doesn't know how to manage her fears and her thinking, she may telephone the police station or the hospitals, or she may get worried and disturb the neighbors and wake up the children—all because of her negative and fearful thinking. If you are negative and frightened all the time, you are afraid of dying, you are afraid of not attaining what you want, and you are afraid of losing what you have. You have so many fears, and fear is the greatest of all enemies.

You think all the time, but you don't yet have a clear philosophy. You should create a clear philosophy of life for yourself that should start with an understanding of your duties, the duties you have assumed in life. You cannot live without doing your duties, so you should study and fully understand the law of karma: Whatever you do, you are bound to receive and reap the fruits of your actions. And since those fruits motivate you to further action, there is no end to the process. You cannot renounce performing your karmas. You have to do even what you call your daily duties: caring for your body, eating food, and going to the bathroom. So there is no such thing as total renunciation of action. But there is a path to freedom—freedom from the bondage of your actions and karma. You can learn to live in the world and yet remain unaffected by it.

The path toward self-realization starts with work. Do your duties. My duty toward my students is to teach them selflessly. If I do not do my duty well, then my conscience will create an inner conflict and I will torment myself. Such conflict within is the source of your misery, especially when it is about how you perform your duties. What I am saying is that you should observe your actions and learn to understand them. What are you doing? You say, "I don't want to do this, but I am doing it," or "I want to sit down, relax, have a cup of tea, and talk to you, but I cannot." This is how you create conflict and division in your own mind. You do an action because you think you cannot live without it, and then you reap the fruit. You are miserable because you are grasping and holding onto the fruits of your actions—you are selfish and possessive. That's why you are miserable. And when you talk of liberation, emancipation, and freedom, that's only a cry for help. When you learn to give to others, then you'll be free.

If you want to live positively and joyfully, learn to give the fruits of your actions to others, and determine that you will not allow yourself to be bothered by anything in the external world. If you do not learn to give, then you are being selfish and negative. A negative person is selfish; a positive person is generous. You cannot rely upon a negative person. There are some people who never come into contact with their positive emotions—they only remain negative all the time. And because of this they are unable to give to others.

So learn to give to your own people, those with whom you live, those who are closest to you. Learn to give spontaneously in your mind, action, and speech. That is your first step to freedom. It is attained when you learn to do your actions with love and learn to give. Love means non-harming, so you should resolve that you will not harm, hurt, or injure your spouse, children, or friends—that means that you love them. The expression of your love is in not harming or hurting others. Love does not consist of telling someone that you love them and cannot live without them—that is mere selfishness. If you love someone, then don't harm or hurt them—that is the real expression of your love.

These days, "stress" is a burning topic. But what is the cause of stress? Your neighbors, family, and work do not create stress for you. Stress results when you feel that you are doing something that you should not do, or when you feel that you are being forced to do what you are doing. Stress also results when you are not able to do what you want to do, and that creates a conflict in your mind.

How are you going to enlighten yourself if you remain caught up in a whirlpool that you are creating for yourself? Most of your miseries are actually created by you, and then you ask God to help you. But if you create misery for yourself, what kind of God will come down and help you? It will never happen, because that misery is being created by you. So decide every morning that no matter what happens, you will not let anything disturb you. If you become emotionally disturbed, then you cannot do anything worthwhile.

We try to look nice for others, but we are actually cheating them—we try to present ourselves as something that we are not. It's good to dress nicely and to have a good haircut, but this has nothing to do with your inner reality. Everyone feels that life is stressful, but they dress themselves up and try to look nice; so everyone has a mask they use to hide how they really are. That adds to the stress.

I remember a situation where a boy was courting a girl. He said to me, "Swamiji, that girl is so beautiful. I cannot live without her. She is very beautiful."

But I said, "Don't marry her," because I felt that his concept of love was not mature.

One day he saw her early in the morning before she had put on her makeup. He came to see me immediately and said, "I don't want to marry her anymore. She's ugly!" His appreciation and admiration of her beauty was gone in one second's time. The girl was sleeping; she got up and went to the door when someone knocked, and then he didn't want to marry her. I told him, "I pity the depth of your love. Do you love only cosmetics?"

Don't become a hypocrite or be dishonest. Try to show and express that which you are. If you feel good and accepting of yourself, that's good; but if you do not feel good or accepting, don't say that you are fine. Even at home you are not completely honest with your family when they ask how you are. And when you are not honest, you create a conflict within yourself. You form a bad habit; you become weak and full of fear; you make yourself insecure.

Of course you don't want to upset others, but forming a habit of acting happy when you are not is like constantly not telling others what is real or the truth. That creates a bad habit—and then it becomes a part of your life. In this way, you never become aware of your real feelings. If you want to be positive without being dishonest, there's another way. You can easily say, "Things will improve," or "God will help us," or many other phrases which will not disturb others. But don't say that you are fine when you are not. You should share your joy and cheerfulness, but that joy should not come through an artificial smile. When you smile like that, it is like slapping your cheeks and then smiling. You should have a genuine smile.

You don't observe within yourself because you are hypnotized by the suggestions of others. Others tell you, "You are like this; you are like that," and you accept such suggestions—and then you become what they have told you. For instance, if you have a problem, everyone will suggest a different solution. Everyone wants to become your teacher. But unfortunately, you have not yet become your own teacher. You do not discover something new for yourself because you are always blasted first by the suggestions you constantly receive from outside yourself.

Your real education begins when you learn to explore and

discover yourself without the opinions of others, when you begin to understand your own thought processes, desires, emotions, and appetites. The day that you learn to see yourself independently, you'll be free.

Slowly, you should learn to be an "insider." An insider is aware and attentive to the reality within. An "outsider" is only aware of the external reality. Don't remain an outsider throughout your entire life. Make gradual progress: at first, you may only be an insider twenty percent of the time and an outsider eighty percent of the time. Slowly, when you go within, you will grow to become fifty percent an insider and fifty percent an outsider. This is a wonderful combination, because you are half there and half here. Before the light of the body extinguishes, learn to focus all your awareness within. Then, you merely leave your shell here. In this way, you will make gradual progress.

Never give up in the face of your own weaknesses. Never think that you cannot do something because you are a woman, for example, or that you are all alone. This is negative thinking. Don't do that to yourself. Do your best and then surrender all your actions and their fruits to the Almighty, the Lord of Life. Pray to him, to the innermost dweller within yourself: "Give me strength so that I can endure this. Give me strength so that I am successful. Give me strength so that I don't forget you." If you ask for that, you'll gain strength. All strength really comes from within; the outside world inspires, but strength comes from within.

If you want to change your personality, and if you are following a true path and you commit a mistake, you'll receive help because of your quest for truth. Your inner world is larger and more powerful than the world you see around you. There is something great inside you. Someone is witnessing your actions, speech, and mind, and that observer is actually the finest part of yourself. The day that you go to that level, you will no longer condemn yourself. You'll no longer find any weakness in yourself. Go there and find that self within. Don't continue to remain lost outside yourself and ignorant of your true and inherent nature.

There is a Sanskrit saying, "If you help yourself, God will help you. But if you do not help yourself, God is not going to help you." The ocean is full of water, and you can draw out as much as you want. There's light everywhere, and nature is everywhere in abundance. You can use the power of nature according to your own needs. You have all the power you need. You simply have to be conscious; you have to be aware of who you are. Becoming free from the bondage of karma is the first step toward freedom.

Chapter 3

PERFECTING THE PERSONALITY

The word "personality" comes from the Greek root, *persona,* or mask, because actors in ancient Greece used masks to show what character they were playing. You too wear masks. They are your personality. Your habit patterns create a mask for you, and that becomes your personality. But who are you really? Who made these masks for you? You are the way you have made yourself. You have manufactured something for yourself to wear. Sometimes the mask exists for defense, or protection; sometimes the mask exists to deflect others; sometimes it is for creative purposes. You use the mask of the personality for many reasons.

You chose these masks. You are your own creation. When you suffer, you sometimes think that your suffering is due to God, but that is a poor philosophy because God never wants anyone to suffer. Why would God be interested in creating suffering? You wanted to be the way you are and that is how you have created yourself, so you should not blame others for your personality or its conflicts.

In reality, you dismiss the fact that your personality is what you have made yourself, and then you say, "This is just the way I am!" or, "God has made me the way I am," which means that you also do not understand the word "God." The word "God" stands for that principle of equality, love, and selfless brilliance—the summum bonum of life. You should not misuse the idea of God to claim that God created you the way you are. You are a spark of the great light; there is no doubt about that. That great light which is within you is actually a nucleus, and this whole universe is its expansion. You'll understand this truth only when you have experienced it.

It is your own actions that make you suffer. These actions can be divided into three classes: past, present, and future. To understand them, imagine you are carrying a quiver of arrows on your shoulder. There is one set of arrows that you have already sent toward the target—they are the actions of the past. Those arrows that you are holding in your hands are present actions, and those arrows that are still in your quiver are future actions. Perhaps you are not happy with some event from your past; perhaps you expected too much of yourself and condemn yourself by thinking that you have not done enough, and constantly repeat the thought that your past actions were not healthy or good. Thus, you have created the habit of condemning yourself—and this creates negativity in your mind. But your present and future actions are still in your hands, and that is where you should focus your mind.

You have the power to change your destiny. You have the power to change your personality. You have the power to change the entire stream of your life and give it a new direction. There is one difficulty in doing this, however, and that is your habit patterns. Your personality is woven by your habit patterns, and your habits are formed because you have repeated some action or thought again and again until you do it unconsciously. Eventually, it becomes a full-fledged habit. When you understand that all your habits are formed by the simple process of repeating some action or thought again and again, then you can learn another process: that of undoing and changing your habits.

I often find that in the schools and colleges you do not learn the technique of how to forget things. You have not learned how to unlearn negative or disturbing things that you have already learned. You do not know how to forget and unlearn. When you want to go to bed to retire and relax, many things are constantly going on in your mind. Your mind is thinking and thinking, and you cannot gain freedom from that process because you have not learned the method of unlearning, of how to be free when you want to be free. When you want to rest, you cannot, because you are still thinking.

The mind is a wall which stands between you and reality. Books can tell you many things, but when you study your own mind, you may discover that today you are at peace and feel that you have conquered your mind, but tomorrow you suddenly lose your temper. Perhaps you say something that is not to be said, or do something that should not be done. You do not know from where this behavior is coming, and you blame others.

In human relationships the most destructive of all weaknesses is the weakness of blaming others. You think, "I am suffering because of you," or, "I am unhappy because of you." You blame others when you are unhappy and expect that others are going to make you happy. But no one has the capacity to do this. It is your own *samskaras*, the impressions stored in the unconscious mind, that make you happy or unhappy. To understand this you have to understand something about the mind/body relationship: If you look at me, and then a few minutes later you look at me again, you will recognize me. This means that your optic nerve conducted an impression of me to your mind, where it was stored, and when you saw me again this impression came forward.

Samskaras are the strong seeds you have sown in your

unconscious mind by your experiences and thoughts. They last for the duration of this lifetime, and according to the sages, they lead to the next birth. They are the powerful motivations that affect the way you function, the way you think and feel—and even the things you desire. All these are due to your samskaras, the "seed memories" of your previous actions, which you have stored in the reservoir within yourself.

The mind has two aspects—conscious and unconscious. The conscious part is only a small part of the totality of mind. It is the aspect that you have been training through your educational system. But you pour all the experiences you have into the unconscious mind. Sometimes, if you do not work with yourself, if you do not sincerely practice to improve yourself and do not really want to change your personality, you feel helpless and at the mercy of your samskaras.

Down deep within you is a basement in which you have stored all the seeds of your samskaras, the bubbles, or impressions, that disturb your behavior and your normal thinking process. Even if your wife, children, and friends tell you not to worry, you cannot stop it. You do it because of your learned habit patterns. Perhaps you have a bad temper; you get angry, and your anger is not controlled anger. You have not learned to discipline yourself, and this is injurious to you. You have to analyze that anger: why do you get so angry that your speech is distorted and you feel different; why do you forget yourself, your duties, and your relationships; and why do you lose your temper and say things that are damaging and injurious?

If you analyze this process, you will find that in the samskaras that you have deposited in the unconscious mind, there are many desires that have not been fulfilled. As a human being you need to have some desires. You cannot live totally without desires. But they should be filtered by the sense of discrimination within you. Your buddhi (intelligence) has the function of judging and deciding which desires are useful. You should learn to develop that function within yourself. Then you can decrease your desires. It is the useless desires that create problems for you, not appropriate or helpful desires.

Once, a journalist asked Mahatma Gandhi how to attain happiness. Gandhi answered, "When you don't have any desires, then you will be happy." Normally, you think, "When I attain God, then I will be happy," but to be practical, you have to recognize that when you don't have any desires, it means that you have fulfilled all your desires, and then you are happy.

So you should develop a sense of discrimination and understanding about what desires are right or helpful to pursue. And you should entertain only those that are right for you and you can fulfill. If you have developed the capacity to discriminate among your desires, then you don't entertain the ones that are injurious to you and drive you crazy or create a state of helplessness. Unfulfilled desires will always lead to a state of unhappiness. For example, perhaps you want to be respected by someone. If this desire exists in you, it will not allow you to be at peace. You may think, "My partner doesn't respect me." Then you waste your time and energy in hoping that other people will respect you and love you. Soon that desire becomes an expectation. In this way, you become dependent on others to fulfill your expectations, and when they are not fulfilled you are miserable. You do nothing for yourself, but you expect things from others.

But others have no capacity to fulfill your expectations; they are your own expectations. The mother of all problems and conflicts lies within you, and that is expecting things from others. And the more you expect from others, the more you are disappointed. You have identified yourself with your negative emotions, thoughts, and traits.

Perhaps you have done something negative in your life, and then decided that you would not do it again. You made an effort, but you still continued to do it. You originally did the action against your own conscience; you knew that you should not have done it, but you did, even though it was against your own personal philosophy. During your life you do many such things, and then you identify with them and form a new, negative personality. You decide that you are a bad person and condemn yourself. You decide that you are weak. You wonder if it is possible for you to be enlightened or to attain a state that is free from all your problems, emotions, pains, and miseries. You are unhappy and helpless. You pray to God to give you strength, but your strength has been diminished by actions that are not in accordance with your ethics or your conscience. With this feeling, you walk the earth constantly depressed and disappointed in life.

You know you have done something that you think was bad. But that doesn't mean you are bad. It was merely a deed, an action. How can you come out of the influence of this regret? You should simply not do the action again, and then you are free—your mind is free. You will not reap the fruits of the action because you are not doing the act. If you are mentally free, you are physically free.

When people say that they condemn themselves, my response is, "Who are you to condemn yourself? Do you belong to yourself or do you belong to God?" If you belong to God, then what right do you have to condemn yourself? You have every right to criticize your actions; your actions are yours. But you belong to God so you don't have the right to condemn yourself.

Negative thoughts often involve going back into the past. You remember the events of the past and then you identify with your past actions. But if you allow yourself to go on thinking in that way you will never come out of the past. And then you will never enjoy either the present or the future. You have to emerge from dwelling on the past. You have to decide that you are neither bad, nor weak, nor limited. The real source of knowledge is within; the world outside only gives you facts to relate to that particular knowledge that is already within you. Never forget that the source of knowledge is within you. You need to learn to help yourself, and you have the capacity to do that by beginning the inward journey.

If you want to fully understand your mind, you will have to eliminate your negative assumption that you are only a small and limited creature. You think of yourself only in limited terms. You habitually identify yourself with your limitations and weaknesses, not with your highest nature. You cannot imagine that someone like you could have a great and powerful mind. So you need to learn to select or reject from among your many thoughts and reject those thoughts that are disturbing to you. But there is a problem or difficulty in doing this. You know what is right and wrong or good and bad for yourself. You know this, so why do you do things that should not be done? The simple answer is that it is due to your habits. Habits are a very strong force in the human mind and personality, but unfortunately you do not appreciate their power.

So do not identify yourself with your past deeds. When you do that, you think, "I did this act the day before yesterday, so I am a bad person." If you think this way, you will not improve. Ramakrishna Paramahansa says, "If you go on thinking that you are bad, bad, bad, then you are bad. Then, you can never improve. You will have to come out of the influences of your past impressions which you carry in your heart and in your unconscious mind."

When you do wrong, and you do not know what you are doing, then you are forgiven. But when you knowingly do something wrong, you are not forgiven and you will reap the consequences. The consequences come through your habit patterns, but you can discipline yourself. Gradually and slowly, you can work with yourself. Don't give up. You'll attain what you want. If you think you are too weak, go to someone who is stronger and they will help you.

In life, there are two processes going on simultaneously: accepting and rejecting things. When you walk, you are rejecting the old space and accepting a new space. When you swim, you push the water back in order to go forward. When you exhale, you reject carbon dioxide and accept fresh air. So learn not to accept the idea that you are a bad person. And do not accept negative feedback. For example, you hear what others say and then you accept their comments. You start to think, "Really, I must be bad. I am not good enough. They say I am bad, so I must be." Something negative has taken control of your life, and so the negative side of your personality has become more powerful than the positive side. You have not worked with your own negative thought processes, and now you are unhappy. This acceptance of others' feedback is not healthy. It can even lead to psychiatric treatment.

When I first visited the United States, the third or fourth day that I was here, I told somebody, "You look beautiful," and she replied, "Oh, you just made my day!" You often react to others' praise this way, and your reaction means that you are constantly craving and needing another's appreciation. Thus, when others tell you that you look beautiful, you accept it, but you did not realize it before. You need others to constantly give you such compliments, and then you become dependent on them. For example, a wife looks to her husband for appreciation, and if he says a kind word to her, she hugs and kisses him. But this dependence on others' support or praise is not dealing with reality; it is merely living on the strength of others' approval and appreciation, and then you develop weak and unreal ways of thinking.

Whatever you do—whether it is the kind of clothes you

wear, the way you walk, or the way you talk—do not do it for others. If you do something just because your neighbor has done it, you become a kind of "reactionary." Something destructive happens to you: You lose touch with yourself and you become a mere reactor to others. Then you don't do what you really value, think, or believe; you do only what others value. And when this happens you no longer live for yourself; you begin to live for others in a negative way. Perhaps your neighbors dislike you, so you dislike the neighbors, and that's how you live your whole life. Then hatred and jealousy become a part of your life.

Your major problem is that you do not fully know, understand, and accept yourself. Thus, you are dependent on the suggestions and support of others. In fact, most of your problems are created for you by those who claim to be your friends. They give you a sickness, and you call it love. And because you are dependent and insecure, you constantly create ego problems with them.

So don't hanker for others' approval or worry about what the world thinks of you—that can become a great complex. Many people behave nicely, but only because they worry about what others will think. That is not good; when you act that way, it means that you have become subject to something external and have become a puppet. If you feel you want to do something from within, and if you go on doing it and are committing a mistake, you can correct it. But what you do only because others want you to, you can never correct. So you should learn to do what you feel. Learn why you feel as you do, and why you like something. If you go on learning and understanding, finally you will learn what is right for you. That which is not wrong is always right.

The difference between an ordinary man and a sage is that the sage is strong from within and does not allow anyone to affect his mind and emotions. The Buddha demonstrated this in the village of Rajgrahi after he left his throne, renounced his kingdom, and went to that small village to perform austerities. Begging helps one to reduce the ego, so he went there to beg for alms. He was a prince, but he wanted to be the world's simplest man.

At that time there were thousands of monks in Rajgrahi. They would stand outside someone's door and chant, "*Narayana, Han,*" which means "Remember God's name." And when villagers heard that, they knew someone had come to the door for *bhiksha* (alms). But almost every third person was a monk, and it became impossible for the villagers to feed them all. One day the Buddha went begging with Ananda, his closest disciple, who used to accompany him. The Buddha always stood quietly outside, but when he arrived at one house, the mother became very angry.

"You are a healthy man, a strong man, a handsome man, standing at our door," she shouted, "and I don't have that much food to give. I have already given away food to many other monks. What shall I give you? I'm only a poor lady. Go away! Don't you have any other place to go?!"

The Buddha smiled gently. Then she said, "Wait, I will give you *bhiksha*," and she picked up the filth from her child, the stool, and offered it to the Buddha, saying, "This is what you deserve!"

The Buddha merely smiled and said simply, "Mother, you can keep that. I don't need it."

Ananda, however, was very angry and shouted, "Woman, you are insulting my lord and master; I'll kill you!"

But the Buddha said to Ananda, "Stop! She wants to give me something, but if I don't need it, I don't take it. So why are you angry?"

This is the important question: When people try to give you their anger or negative feedback, why do you accept it? If someone says that you are bad, why do you accept that? You accept it because you do not have self-confidence; you do not accept yourself; you do not know deep inside that you are good. And because you do not really know yourself, you have formed the habit of depending on the judgments of others. But in your heart of hearts, you should never accept these negative suggestions. They can create a serious problem for you.

You can go to a therapist, and the therapist may explore your problem and tell you the reason for your unhappiness. But if you continue your bad habits, then you will create that misery for yourself again and again. You need to learn to be free from your own habit patterns. Your mind travels in particular grooves that you have created for yourself, and your mind refuses to come out of those grooves. The real experts, the sages and teachers, say that to change you have to create new grooves in your mind. And when the mind starts traveling in new grooves, then your habit patterns will change because your thoughts will change, and then your personality will also change.

You can gain conscious control over yourself through effort. Human beings have the power to make that effort; they can change their personality and utilize the immense wealth, power, and brilliance buried within themselves. Once you learn to go to the inner chamber of your being, you can do that. If you first decide to change, and then learn how to determine within that you will not repeat something negative, you can change your personality.

But if you accept the idea that you cannot change, then you cannot do anything in life. You will be a total failure; then you cannot be creative and you cannot improve. If this is how you live, then what is the use of living? Such a life is boring and becomes a burden to you. But when you learn to work with yourself gently and gradually, you can change your whole being if you really want to, because you can change your masks. Even though the masks that you wear have been chosen and made by you, you can change them and make your personality a pleasant one. So work with your samskaras. If you make a sincere effort, you will learn that all your actions give you their fruits; there is no such thing as an action that does not give a fruit.

Every action has its reaction. No one can overturn this law. When you make a sincere effort, you sometimes feel that you are not improving, but that is not possible. If you do not see progress, then it may be that you are not making an effort truthfully, with full determination, and with all your might. The moment you start to do that, you will find there is a dynamic change in your thinking and behavior.

You can gain freedom from the thinking process which distorts your life by understanding how to train yourself and then going in a different direction. But you must really want to do this. That inner method of self-change is not taught in the external world. You will have to discover it for yourself by understanding a method called "journeying within." Through this method you come to understand yourself and the various levels of your life by studying each level, one after another. And in this way you will learn how to go inside.

First, you need to understand yourself, and understanding yourself means knowing that while the body is subject to change, death, and decay, the soul is not. The soul is immortal. You need to understand your internal states. You need to observe how your mind functions, and to consider the reasons why others do not think the same way you think.

Do the following experiment for just a day or two: Use that great power that is your inherent power—the power called love. Learn to express yourself in such a way that you don't hurt, injure, or harm others. Learn to give. Often you hurt others merely for the sake of your own selfish ego. Yoga science makes the true meaning of love clear when it describes the practice of *ahimsa* (not harming, hurting, or injuring others). If you learn to practice ahimsa, then you are practicing love in your daily life, and the practice of love does not mean being selfish. How many times a day do you have the desire to give the wealth and bounty you have to others—even to those who are related to you? The ability to give to outsiders develops later on. Ahimsa should be practiced first with those close to you, and when you have learned to enjoy giving, a time will come when you can give without any reservation.

All the great men and women who have lived on this earth have been selfless and desireless; they lived to serve and help others. They knew that the only way to freedom is to learn to give. This is the law of life. So you should continue to do the experiment with yourself, and every time you do, you will find that you are growing and growing. Eventually your growth will lead you to a state and a height in which you are free from all desires that are selfish. The desire to help others, to serve others, to serve the nation and humanity—these are great desires. When all your small desires are swallowed by the great desires, then your life will be like that of a saint, and you will find that you have become entirely different.

A good person really lives. One who is not healthy or helpful for himself cannot be healthy and helpful to others. One who suffers from himself cannot love others, and cannot perform actions that are selfless. These people create a whirlpool for themselves; they cannot cross the mire of delusion that arises in their own mind or go beyond. They cannot rise. But in all the great cultures of the world there have been extraordinary men who can be examples for you. Sometimes they were crucified, killed, rebuked, or stoned, but always it was for the sake of others—never for themselves. Petty men die for themselves and for their own petty desires; great men die because they want to serve humanity. Both die, but there is a difference in their dying and their living.

History tells us that even the worst man can become a

sage, and there are many examples of those who have transformed themselves. That is what happened to the Indian sage
Valmiki, who was originally a robber. One day a swami was
going down the path through a dense forest. He did not own
anything but a water pot, but Valmiki captured the swami,
snatched his water pot, and beat him. The swami then said,
"Son, listen to me first, and then you can kill me if you want!
Why are you doing this? Do you think you are doing it for your
wife or children? Why have you formed such a bad habit? Go
and ask your wife and children if they are willing to share in
the fruits of the bad karma you have created for doing these
deeds." Valmiki went and asked first his wife and then his sons
if they would share the fruits of his karma with him. They
laughed and said that his bad karma was his, and why should
they share it? Valmiki then understood the truth and changed
his ways. In time, he became an enlightened sage.

Whether you look at the Sufi tradition, Chinese history,
or Japanese history, you will find that in all of them great
people have also transformed themselves. You will find that
even though they were not at first either good or wise (in fact,
they may even have been the worst people) these great human
beings were able to change their entire character and
personality. Even murderers and habitual criminals have
changed their personality.

Whether or not you are educated and cultured, your
conscience comes forward and asks you, "Why are you doing
this?" You don't need anyone outside yourself to tell you that
something is right or wrong for you; you know it. Before St.
Paul became a great spiritual leader, he was Saul, a very bad
man. He was transformed on the way to Damascus because his
conscience began to ask him, "Why are you doing these things?
Why aren't you walking on the path of righteousness?" And
because he listened to his conscience, he was transformed.

You have two different kinds of resources: the external,

superficial resources, which are momentary and ever changing; and the internal resources, which are permanent and unchanging. External resources help you to accomplish external things, but only internal resources really help you and make you strong. You are fully equipped with all the resources and power that you need, but usually you do not tap them because you have formed a habit of seeking help in the external world. Such reliance is not safe; it's merely a crutch. Great people learn through their mistakes. The more you rely on yourself and learn from your mistakes, the stronger you become.

If you commit a mistake, then learn from it. To commit a mistake is human, but to go on committing mistakes is a sin. Once you know that something is injurious for you, you can decide not to continue to commit that mistake, because it does not allow you to grow and it does not change your personality or make you happy. Do not give up on yourself by deciding that you cannot improve. The moment you decide that you are not going to repeat actions that are unhealthy for you or your growth, then you are free.

You are not any worse than Saul. If Saul could become St. Paul, then you can also transform yourself. History tells you that you have the power, capacity, and ability to change yourself—provided you decide to do it. When you have learned how to decide, how to make a resolution, when you work to increase your determination, then you can change your personality. You can become a great sage like Saul. That is the path of changing the personality.

Observe your own thinking processes and your internal states, but don't accept negative suggestions from any quarter. Certainly, you commit mistakes, and you should learn to rectify those mistakes. You become free by not repeating a mistake, so do not brood over it. Through the power of prayer you can pour out all your superficial tendencies of mind—your faults and desires—and try to be in touch with the deepest and finest level of your being, the center of consciousness within. You can say, "O Lord, I want the energy to handle this situation." And you can do it if you have learned to rely upon your internal resources.

Your personality can be changed. In this lifetime you can attain the highest rung of life, a state that is free from pain and misery. Don't postpone this as you postpone the other joys of your life. Enlightenment, that state of freedom from pain and misery, is your birthright. It is not something acquired or new—it is already there. You can realize that state. So learn to work with yourself to remove the barriers to your growth. Learn to change your habits, and thus purify and perfect your personality. This is your challenge—to transform your own personality!

Chapter 4

THE NATURE OF POSITIVE AND NEGATIVE EMOTIONS

If I move my hand and make a certain gesture as I speak, what prompts me to do that? Most of our gestures are unconscious, so perhaps as I speak, some part of my body is moving. The body has a language of its own, which we call "body language." It creates such gestures because all its actions are governed and controlled by our thoughts. This is an important point: your actions are controlled by, and are the result of, your thoughts, both conscious and unconscious. Any movement means that some thought that exists in the mind is being expressed.

Everything your body does has a meaning: if you overeat, you burp; if your body aches or is stiff, you will move in a certain way. When your body is in pain, others can tell from your movements that there is something wrong. Your gestures are totally influenced by your thought processes. Actually, the English word "man" is related to the Sanskrit word, *mana*, which means "mind," and to fully know and understand yourself as a human being, you must first understand your own mind by studying yourself.

For example, you want to be loved all the time. It is true that love is the Lord of Life, but observe what happens inside you if you hate one person and love someone else. Notice the process: your hatred is intense for the one you dislike, but your love for the other is not of such intensity. You actually "love" your enemy more than your friend because your mind is focused on your enemy all the time. You think of your enemy frequently; you hate your enemy constantly; you are angry with your enemy all the time. So much of your energy is diverted toward your animosity—who do you really love? You devote more time to your enemy than to your lover.

Unfortunately, in human life your hatred goes to deeper levels within you than your love. You want to direct your energy toward the center of your love and not toward hatred, but the opposite happens because you do not know the method of directing that mental power and energy called "right thinking." Instead, you repeat and intensify negative emotions until they become a powerful habit.

Nobody likes to think in this negative way. But even if you go to a temple or a church, you still think of your enemy. Wherever you go—even in bed with your sweetheart—you think of your enemy. How powerful your hatred is! The force of hatred in your mind is so powerful because you have never really trained yourself—you have not yet learned to direct the energy of the thinking process.

A writer once beautifully said, "If a good thought is not brought into action, it's either a kind of treachery or an abortion." This means that that which is good within you should be expressed. But what is a "good thought"? A good thought is that which makes you creative, a thought that does not create conflicts within you. A good thought is that which makes you peaceful, tranquil, balanced, happy, and joyous. Such a thought should not be allowed to die unexpressed within yourself, nor should it remain asleep or dormant within. It should be expressed through your mind, action, and speech.

But there is something even more powerful beneath the thought level, and that is the emotional power within you, the deeper part of your mental process. Emotions are very powerful, and if you can use that emotional power, you can attain the highest state of ecstasy in a second's time. But if you mingle and blend that emotional power with your negative habit patterns, then you are gone! Then no one can protect you from yourself. An immense resource is within you, but it is either not being utilized at all, or it is being badly utilized. You are using your emotional power to form bad habit patterns.

For example, you have everything that you need around you; there is someone to tell you, "Honey, I love you." Your child says, "Mom, I love you," and yet you are not at peace. This is not due to your thinking patterns alone, because beneath your thinking process lies something even deeper than thoughts—the power of emotion. In your daily life, among your friends and families, both at home and at work, you sometimes realize, or others tell you, that you are too emotional, that you are not emotionally balanced. When this happens, it is because you have not properly understood or organized your emotional life.

Emotions can be powerful in either positive or negative ways. Perhaps, for example, you are driving your car and you suddenly see that a small puppy is caught in a bush and is crying helplessly. The puppy does not belong to you, but if you are in touch with your positive emotions at that time, you may stop and try to help it. Such emotions can lead you to creativity and positive action, but there are also negative emotions, which can lead you to disaster and destroy your life.

For example, when you are upset, disorganized, or emotionally out of control, you say things that you don't really mean. Later, you're sorry, but what prompted you to say that negative thing in the first place? You never really meant to hurt anybody, so then you apologize to those you love. "I'm sorry," you say, "I didn't mean to hurt you. I love you, and I'm sorry I said that." But the next day you repeat the same behavior, because you do not understand your own emotions. You need to understand what prompted you to become wild and to have that emotional outburst.

Often, you weaken yourself in daily life. You leave for work smiling, and then suddenly something happens on your way to work and you become sad. That's life. You are experiencing the changes and the ups and downs of life all the time. To deal with these changes, you must develop your determination that you will not be emotionally disturbed by events and will not do anything that hurts or harms others.

There have been many great sages, such as Chaitanya Mahaprabhu, Ramakrishna Paramahansa, Saint Bernard, and Saint Teresa, who learned to tap their emotional power in a creative way. They used their emotional power rather than the power of mind. This is called "the path of the heart." To follow the path of the mind is very dangerous; it's like the sharp edge of a knife. If you make a mistake with your mind, you will be destroyed, but if you learn to use your emotions positively, you can attain the highest of joys and happiness.

Chaitanya Mahaprabhu came into contact with that emotional power directly, and he channeled it through chanting. When you cry, which is another way people express emotions, you experience pain and misery, but when you chant you are in joy. Using your emotions in a negative way means crying and being miserable. Using your emotion in a creative way means chanting, singing, making poems, and dancing. But actually, it's the same emotional power.

The book of wisdom, the Upanishads, the most ancient of the scriptures in the library of man, says: "O man, if you truly understand that power within you, then you know that you are God yourself. If you do not yet understand who you really are, then you are still a brute, and when you understand who you are a little bit, then you are a human being."

You each have all three of these qualities within you: the divine, the human, and the animal. When you experience your animal emotions, then you suddenly forget your children, your husband or wife, and your friends. You become wild and forget your responsibilities and relationships. And when you forget your responsibilities, you are not in touch with your internal states.

This does not mean that you are a bad person, or have ugliness inside you; it means that you have not yet learned to organize, direct, and lead that great emotional power. Someone who knows how to do this can attain in a short time the same height of ecstasy as that achieved by yogis who do intense practices for many years to attain *samadhi*. Both processes are the same, provided you know how to channel your emotions and have learned how to go beyond the mire of delusion created by your own mind and its thinking process. This is possible when you understand the origins of your emotions.

First, you must understand the negative emotions, know what they are and from where they arise. The spiritual scriptures of the ancient sages analyzed these negative emotions and categorized them. The first, they say, is *kama*, the mother of all other desires. Kama is the prime desire. From it arise all the others. Kama gives rise to the desire to satisfy or gratify the senses; it also gives rise to the desire to help others selflessly. Kama motivates you to do anything and everything. But it is blind desire: it has no sense of discrimination, no judgment, no understanding. It motivates you to do something just to fulfill that desire—simply because it exists.

When kama is not fulfilled, you get angry and frustrated—that is *krodha*, the emotion of anger. When you are angry, then you are completely blind. If you compare yourself to a dog, you will realize that even a dog never loses its temper in the way that you do. When you are frustrated, when your desires are not fulfilled, you can even hurt your children or your wife—those you love so much.

Unfulfilled desire leads to anger. When you get angry it is because something is not fulfilling your desires, and in this fashion you get angry a thousand times a day. A desire creates expectation, and that expectation is strong, so there is constant anger. And when you express your anger it wrecks your nervous system. You start trembling when you are angry; you lose your balance; you lose your tranquility. A complete and accurate definition of anger is the emotion resulting from unfulfilled desires that you have not learned how to arrange, to pacify, or to understand. Thus, anger means that you have some desire that needs to be understood and resolved.

If, however, your desire has been achieved and kama has been fulfilled, then pride, or *muda*, results. Your mind thinks, "I have achieved my desire!" This is intoxicating, and when you are under the influence of this intoxication you do not think clearly and you behave badly. Thus, when the desire is fulfilled you become proud, but if it is not fulfilled then you become angry.

Because of this, you need to be careful to observe yourself clearly. When a desire is fulfilled, you should observe whether it feeds your pride, and if it is not fulfilled, observe whether it feeds your anger. You have to watch yourself carefully for these two reactions.

Now comes the next step in the analysis of negative emotions: when a desire is fulfilled and you attain what you long for, then you become attached to it. This attachment is called *moha*, the sense of "This is mine!" Once you attain something, you become attached to it and you want to keep it; you want to repeat the experience, and you fear losing it. But there is an irony in life: When you say, "This is mine," the object actually is not yours; on the other hand, when you claim, "This is not mine," then actually it is yours. You'll constantly observe this in life. "This body is mine," you say, but you cannot keep it from death and decay. You make such false claims your whole life. You live with these false claims because you are attached to them. Sometimes you become overwhelmed with pride for all your achievements or accomplishments. Sometimes you become disturbed emotionally because certain important desires of your desire-world have not been fulfilled.

Then comes the next step: greed, or *lobha*. When you are attached to something, you become greedy. If your desire is fulfilled, you compare yourself with others and think, "I now have it, and you don't have it. I have it and I am proud of it! This is mine because I have it. It is not yours." This is lobha, or greed. Lobha motivates you to feel, "This is mine and I don't want to share it with you. It's my house. My house has twelve rooms, I have only one child, and most of the rooms are empty, but I won't allow you to stay here. It's my house." That is greed. It further separates you from others.

This greed is never fulfilled, no matter what you do. Once you are attached to something, you can never have enough. The fire of greed is horrible. The fire of greed is so intense that you cannot believe its destructiveness—it can even make you sick. There are actually diseases in which greed and longing lead to physical illness. Such an emotion can make you obsessed with something.

When you become greedy, you also become jealous of others and feel insecure. You start comparing your home with the one someone else owns, and then you become jealous. You think, "Does someone have a better house? Oh, no, my house is much better." You begin to compare yourself with others, and then you become puffed up with pride, and you go on living this way, feeding your ego. On the other hand, if you feel that your home is not so nice, you identify with feelings of inadequacy and depression.

You constantly compare yourself with others. What is that thing called "beauty" that you feel so insecure and worry so much about? You are the only one, a unique entity created by Providence. There is no duplication or repetition in the world, so if everything is unique, then who is beautiful and who is ugly? Everything is beautiful! To think that something is beautiful and something different is ugly are ideas you have superimposed on reality. They occur only in your thinking. You judge that one thing is good and another is bad, but such concepts are superimpositions by your mind, by your thinking, and by your impoverished philosophy of life.

The next and sixth major stream of emotion is ahamkara, the sense of "I-am-ness." This is the faculty of the mind which you have constantly been adoring, revering, and worshipping—the ego. This little "I," which you use every day to refer to yourself and not to others, becomes the center of your life. The word that you use again and again in your daily life, "I," becomes the center of your awareness. You say, "I am doing this; I am not doing that; I do not want to do this." All this is the work of ahamkara. You have created a fortress; you have created a barrier with your own ego, and then you do not know how to come out of it in order to know the highest reality. You use all your differences, your defense mechanisms, to protect yourself and your ahamkara.

You need to understand what ahamkara does for you: the sense of I-ness prompts you to live on the earth and to have a particular individuality. Because of ahamkara, you are an individual. But ahamkara also separates you from the whole. When a wife and husband, two lovers, touch a peak that is beyond ahamkara, that is real joy, but ahamkara itself will never give you joy; instead, it will contract your personality. It enables you to be an individual, but it will never give you joy.

You only attain joy when you completely forget ahamkara, when you are no longer limited by ahamkara. But how is it possible for you to live without a sense of I-ness? That's not possible, so it is better to "polish" your ahamkara. Just as you polish your shoes and use them every day until eventually they are worn out, so should you polish your ahamkara—your ego.

All your prayers, all your loves, all your concerns, all your friendships—anything that you consider important in your life—you do because of ahamkara. You think that you love your husband and he thinks that he loves you, but really you each love your own ahamkara. That's why you love others. There is a beautiful saying in Sanskrit, which is translated, "Why do you love your wife, your children, and others? For yourself. For if you yourself did not exist, how could you love anybody?" If you love others for the sake of their *atman* (pure consciousness), that is very good, but usually, you only love them for the sake of your ahamkara.

In most of what you do, you do not do the action for the sake of the action alone. You do not genuinely love someone, or pray to God, or do any good thing—that is the expression of your ahamkara. A rich man's ahamkara is to give donations and to feel proud of his generosity. The rich man doesn't really want to give even a penny; he is greedy, but he wants even more to satisfy his ahamkara. You all want to satisfy your ahamkara. Ahamkara is the great fortress that you have created for yourself; it locks you in and others out. But you can polish your ego and use up the ahamkara.

Thus, there are six main streams of emotions: desire (kama), anger (krodha), pride (muda), attachment (moha), greed (lobha), and the sense of I-ness (ahamkara). Two are primary: kama and ahamkara. Kama is the prime desire, and ahamkara is the sense of "I," that which makes you think, "I am this. This is mine. This is not mine. This is mine and that is yours."

From where do these six streams of emotions come? They must flow from someplace, since they are not the result of your divine nature. This is an important subject. The origin of these streams is in the four primitive fountains of emotion. If you learn this lesson well, it will help you in all areas of life. The four primitive fountains are the source of all emotions.

What are these primitive fountains? They are food, sex, sleep, and self-preservation. All human beings and all creatures have these urges. There is not a big difference between human beings and animals in these urges. In fact, seat your dog in front of you, and you will find that in some ways you are inferior. If the dog was trained not to eat a dog biscuit, it leaves the biscuit there. But you don't have such self-control; any time you want to eat, you eat.

If you eat unhealthy or bad food, then how can you create good and positive emotions? If you eat "junk food," it creates indigestion and many ill effects for your body. Then how do you expect to have creative and positive emotions? We're not talking about vegetarianism versus eating meat; being a vegetarian is not necessary. But if you are talking about creative emotions, then you'll have to understand something: If you throw a piece of meat on the earth, it will not grow meat; it will only be a source of germs and bacteria. It is dead and lacks a certain life force. But if you throw down some grain or seeds, they will sprout and eventually grow other grains. So there is a difference in the quality of these foods, and you should think about that.

Just as imbalanced food can create many emotional disasters and have many negative effects on your life, so also does sex play a part in your emotional balance. If the role of sex is not understood, it has a mysterious power in your life. I have observed that most people are controlled to some degree by the sexual urge. You need to understand the difference between the urge for food and the urge for sex. You must eat food to remain healthy; if you don't eat food for several days, then you won't feel the sexual urge. This means that food itself has an influence on the sexual urge. Food has a direct effect on your body; the body's needs are the most important part of your desire for food.

Sex does not work like that. Sexual desire occurs first in your mind, and if the mind doesn't feel the desire, then you won't experience it physically. When you're attracted to someone physically, you say, "I like you," because such sexual urges originate in your mind and then express themselves through the body. The desire for food, however, originates in the body, and then affects your mind.

Next, there is another urge: the urge for sleep. Even if you are allowed to eat what you want, and to have sex when you want, if you are deprived of sleep you will become crazy and unbalanced and won't be able to live. So the process of sleep should also be well understood. Sleep has many stages and levels: just as you go from your living room to your kitchen, and then from the kitchen to the bedroom, so also do you go through stages of sleep.

One stage in this process is the dreaming process. You have some faint memories and some distorted memories that come to you while you are asleep, and these are your dreams. For you, there is no doubt that they are therapeutic, but for yogis they are not therapeutic. For yogis, the small amount of time available for sleep would be reduced and robbed by dreaming, so they don't allow dreams to invade their sleep. Dreaming is a necessity for normal people, but there is a state of deep sleep that exists when there is no content in the mind at all. You can go there during meditation, and if you learn the method of meditation that can lead you to willful rest, then you won't need to sleep so much.

As far as scientific findings are concerned, no one can really maintain deep sleep for more than three consecutive hours. Actually, you sleep eight hours as a kind of tradition: it's night, there's no light outside, so you go to bed. Throughout the night you wake and think, "I did not hear the alarm yet, so I'll go to sleep again," or you wake up and think, "No one called me yet, so I'll sleep some more." You have created this conditioning in your mind, so that you are in bed for no real reason, tossing and turning. You have formed a bad habit about how you handle your sleep.

The fourth primitive urge is self-preservation. This means that you always desire to maintain and protect yourself. For example, you are afraid of dying. You worry that you might die, or that someone might hurt you, and you wonder who is going to look after you. Because of this negative thought pattern, you experience fear and become a champion of negative thinking. This is the result of the urge for self-preservation.

The body is subject to change, death, and decay, but the soul is immortal. This is a fact accepted all over the world by all the great cultures. If this is true, then where lies the problem? Once you understand that the body perishes and the soul is immortal, then where is the trouble? The trouble lies in your mind—that which stands between the body and the soul. When you learn to surrender yourself, however, to surrender this individual self to the Divine, then you are free. The happiest person in the world is one who is fearless; a fearless person is one who has no conflicts within or without; and one who has no conflicts is balanced.

The four urges for food, sex, sleep, and self-preservation are the root causes for all emotions. And because of this, learning to skillfully balance and channel these urges is an important step on the spiritual path. So when you begin to work with your emotions you should be systematic. First, discover why you become emotional. The cause of emotion is never from deep within you; it is always a reaction to things from without. Something happens externally and then you become emotional—angry or sad. There is some situation outside yourself, and when you react to it, that makes you emotional. You become emotional because you have not yet correctly arranged or understood your relationships with the external world.

Perhaps you cannot deal with certain problems or conflicts at home, and so you go to study with a swami or a yogi, or you start doing *japa* (the repetition of mantra). Avoiding the emotional issue is not going to help you. Instead of dealing with the conflict or issue, you look for answers outside yourself—and of course you don't succeed. But if you remain careful with your emotions, and learn how to go through the ups and downs of life and still remain balanced, then you will not suffer from this kind of conflict. In fact, even some of the diseases that you experience are the result of negative emotions that you do not yet recognize—nor are their causes understood even by medical science.

So learn to understand the origins of your emotions, the places from where these emotions spring. Perhaps you know that you should be nice to your wife, and be gentle, kind, and loving to her. Yet you suddenly become emotional, and you yell or hit her, which you never meant to do. If you continue doing that, you are sick, and if you are sick, you need therapy. Therapy means the process of learning how to be normal and balanced, and to attain that normalcy, you need a kind of therapeutic understanding.

If you ask how one becomes normal, there are several important points which you need to understand. If you work with yourself on these points you will benefit, and if you are in therapy, your therapist will be amazed to see how much progress you have made. In fact, all therapists and teachers should teach their students how to regulate the four primitive fountains: the desires for food, sex, sleep, and the urge for self-preservation. They are the very basis of all problems.

First of all, many problems arise because of the issue of food and how we manage our need for food. If you eat imbalanced and unhealthy food, you will soon become emotionally imbalanced because you are not supplying the necessary nutrients to your body. Thus, you can analyze emotional disease and discover its relationship to food. If you do not supply the proper diet to your body, your body will demand it. Ask those who suffer from diabetes how depressed they are: for them, there is nothing good in life. You supply a bad diet to your body because of your bad habits, because of the appetites that you have acquired.

We eat food because of our acquired tastes. No one eats food as it is, in pure form. No one tastes the food as it is. Certainly, we should cook and bake food, but unless we put in spices or ingredients that have no nutrients, we do not want to eat it. Thus, we acquire certain food and appetite habits which are not healthy. This is the influence of our culture. We do not eat good and healthy food; we do not supply our bodies with the kind of food which is needed by the body and which the body demands. Instead, we feed the body junk food, and this results in many problems.

Whatever you eat, the right kind of diet should be supplied to the body. To be overweight means that you are overeating, so the first question is, why do you overeat? This often happens because you are not supplying a proper diet to the body. Your body is demanding food because something is missing, and so you gain weight. Those who want to lose weight will find that if you supply the proper diet to your body, you won't need to try to lose weight in any way; your weight will be in accordance with your body. You gain weight because you are not supplying the proper diet. So try to understand the nature of the body and your dietary system. You should regulate your food intake and teach your children to do so. And if you eat regularly at the same time, and chew your food well in a calm atmosphere, it helps the system to function.

Any urge that is incorrectly expressed will create stress. If you are not hungry and you force yourself to eat, you are overeating, and it will create stress. If you don't really understand the goal of sexuality, but you do sex to try to release tension or satisfy your ego, that will create stress for you because you are doing something without the right attitude. Eating food or engaging in sexuality without the right attitude will not give you satisfaction; it will not give you any real joy.

Many people do not understand the nature of the sexual urge, the purpose of sexual relationships, or how to manage their sexuality so that it does not create obstacles on the spiritual path. Just as there is a purpose for eating food, a purpose for sleeping, and a purpose for your fears about your safety, there is also a purpose for sexuality. To make progress on the path of spirituality you need to understand this urge, its purpose, and how to satisfy it.

Just as you should learn how to have good and healthy food—which means fresh, nutritious, well-balanced food—so should you also learn something about how to skillfully handle the sexual drive. This is an art that's not taught by parents or schools. In ancient times, the *rishis* (seers) used to teach people these things and impart the kind of training that would help you to understand what sex means to you in your spiritual life. Without such an understanding, everyone in the world thinks of sex all the time, but they don't understand how to handle it. For many people, both food and sex are equally out of balance.

The sexual urge does not start through the body. Sexuality starts in the mind. Food is a necessity of the body first, and then of the mind. Sex is a necessity of the mind first, and then it is expressed through the body. Those who are sexually compulsive or obsessive have something wrong on the mental/emotional level. There is something wrong with their habit patterns, or there is an ego problem. This can be analyzed and understood. If you regulate your diet and the rest of the primitive fountains, then you can become your own therapist. You can learn something from your internal therapist; you can learn to discipline yourself and do things at the right time.

When you have a spouse or a partner, you do not go with another partner. This is part of what is meant by regulation of the sexual urge. You should also regulate the temporal aspect of your behavior—the times in which you do things. Don't just decide to have sex the moment that you come home—learn to prepare yourselves for the experience. Sometimes a woman does not feel prepared for what her partner wants because sexual desire does not originate in the body; it originates in the mind and is then expressed through the body. Sexual desire has nothing to do with virility or strength; it has to do with emotions and the way you channel and express your emotions. So you should have an understanding of your partner's feelings so that you are not disappointed in your expectations of the relationship.

The reason for sexual relationships is for their joy, but you need to understand the higher goals beyond that goal. In India, we often use a Persian word *shadi*, which means "happiness" or "marriage." When you get married, your partner gives you a ring, which symbolizes something: the two separate ends of the same piece of metal come together and that becomes a perfect complete circle, a ring. Your purpose is to be united to the end of life, and that is a kind of completion or happiness.

So why do human beings become so involved in sexual desire and activity that they think only about that? One reason is that there are two varieties of joy in life. One is called *vishaya ananda*, the kind of joy you obtain when you do sex. Such joy does not last long. You want it to last forever;

you don't want merely five minutes of joy and then the sadness that you experience, but that is what happens to you.

Anything in the world that you enjoy, or that gives you joy, does not last for long. Such joy is fleeting: the object that gives you joy or pleasure, the object which becomes a reason for you to live or act—that object itself changes. There is no object on the earth that does not change, that does not go through the process of change, death, and decay. So it is impossible for such objects to give you lasting joy. You cannot count on them.

Your relationships with the objects of your sexual desire also change, and when you remain floating on the level of sexual joy alone and fail to understand that there is something deeper in a human being—when you don't understand your life on the deeper levels, and when you do not communicate with another beyond the level of the body—that causes problems. Such relationships do not last for very long because a human being is really seeking that joy and happiness which is perennial and constant.

You do not know how to attain that perennial happiness because when you examine and experience the joys of the world, deriving joy from first one source and then another source, going from one object to another, you are disappointed. Finally, you turn within. Then you go to the subtler realms and seek to understand the meaning of life, and you learn that it is not possible for you to attain that perennial happiness and joy in the external world, with such fleeting objects. When you go beyond these objects, then you finally find joy in the center of consciousness within.

You also need to deal with the sleep urge. Sometimes in the morning you will realize that you have not slept well—you feel tired and lazy. On days that you are fully rested, you don't feel that way. But sometimes your sleep is robbed or disrupted by some unconscious agony, some thought or fear. The day after that happens, you'll be tired, but the day after you have fully rested will be different. So it is better for you to sleep after doing a little bit of relaxation and breathing practices. Then you'll have a complete rest.

You may sometimes wonder how yogis can do without sleep. It's not magic; it's that they are relaxed all the time, so why would they need more relaxation? Presently, you need relaxation because you are always on the go, physically and mentally, but if you learn to meditate and really rest, you won't need as much sleep. So you should also regulate your sleep schedule. Yogis reduce the amount of sleep to two and a half hours, and finally to no sleep. They call it "sleepless sleep," and they go to a state of deep meditation instead of sleep. When meditation becomes your whole life, then this change takes place naturally.

I recommend that those who are really meditators learn to wake up at three o'clock. That time of the morning is called *brahmamuhurta*. When you learn to wake at a specific time, then you will also learn how to go to sleep—true, willful sleep—when you want. Then you decide, "I will get up at three o'clock, so now I have to sleep," and you will simply go to sleep. After all, everything that you do can and should come under your conscious control. Presently you are not under your own conscious control, but under the control of your unconscious. Your goal should be to train yourself to be under your conscious control. This is an important process.

There are two types of sleep. One is the sleep that makes you unconscious, that which you think of as sleep. But that unconscious sleep is not really healthy. Just as eating junk food unconsciously is not healthy, so, too, is unconscious sleep not healthy. It helps in one regard, but not in the deepest way, because even in unconscious sleep a part of the mind still remains awake. Perhaps you are sleeping and suddenly somebody touches your body. Even though you are asleep you will brush their hand away, because at some level, your mind is still alert.

Thus, even when you go into a state of deep sleep, a part of the mind remains unrested. What are you going to do with that aspect of mind? You never learn to work with it or develop it; that's why you need to learn relaxation and meditation, so that you can consciously give rest to that part of the mind which is never rested. That is why I tell you to meditate. It's important to do that.

There is also a type of conscious sleep you can learn that is called "sleepless sleep." The sages say that a fool goes to sleep, and comes out a fool, but if a fool goes into meditation he comes out a sage. That's the difference—a fool goes into meditation, and he changes; he comes out a sage. Meditation is a conscious habit, while sleep is unconscious. Meditation gives complete rest to both the conscious and unconscious mind, while sleep gives rest to only the conscious mind. Meditation is important in order to provide complete rest for your body and mind.

In a healthy lifestyle you should have time for exercise, breathing practices, and meditation. You should also understand that you were born, and anything that is born is sure to die. Brooding on death and creating fear is not a helpful thing to do. Sooner or later everything changes and everything dies. You will lose only your body, which dies and decays. So why should you be afraid? Again and again you need to remind your mind of this because you have not been taught to do so; you have been taught to look after yourself fearfully. People said, "Don't go here, you will fall. Don't go there, you will have an accident. Don't go here, someone will kill you." All those negative suggestions are stored in your mind, and thus you become afraid. But most of the fears in your mind are imaginary.

You analyze many things in your life, but you never

analyze your own fears. You will understand this point more clearly in this way: The sense of self-preservation is the highest fountain in us. We seek to protect ourselves all of the time. Consider a reflex action: if I throw something at you, you protect your head with your arms. All the time you are afraid; fear is a major part of your life. In your entire life, your major motivation is fear, yet you never try to examine your fears. You should sit down and ask your mind what your fears are. If you do that, you'll discover that all your fears are imaginary—all are the result of your imagination.

Your imagination creates an image within, but you receive that imagine from outside. There is actually no fear inside you. If you experience fear, you have accepted some image from outside and superimposed it on your mind—and then you hold it, love it, think of it, and become part of it. That is your imagination—that is what you are doing to yourself. Then you condemn yourself for your fears. Why should you condemn yourself? Throw away that superimposition, and you are free. Don't allow your mind to condemn yourself.

The purpose of fear is to lead you to question and understand why you have that fear in the first place. Many fears remain buried within you, and you never really examine them, so you remain at their mercy. In fact, you are afraid to examine your fears, but you should learn to examine each fear, one by one, and to encounter it, and then you will be free of its control. This process is very important. Every human being has certain fears.

For example, one day in Dehra Dun, I was staying at the government house because there were no rooms elsewhere. A great and well-known woman, who was a world leader, arrived the same evening and was staying in another suite. She was famous for her courage and power. She was not afraid of guns, and had even gone to battlefields where journalists and others were afraid. She was so brave that she inspired others. But that night at twelve o'clock she began shouting and crying in her room. So I went out into the hallway and I said, "My sister, what's wrong? Why are you upset?"

And she said, "I have a serious problem."

I said, "Tell me what's wrong or I will break down the door."

She said, "Don't do that!"

I replied, "Then open it!"

And she said, "I can't! There is a spider on the doorknob!" So even that brave woman was afraid of spiders.

Another time, an attorney from Washington, D.C.—a strong, healthy, happy person who helps make legislation in Congress—went to Rishikesh with some people and stayed in one of the outside dormitories, where many people have stayed. It's a clean and comfortable place, but one night the attorney started screaming, "There is a lizard in here!" In tropical countries like India, there are small lizards everywhere, but they are harmless. They don't bite or cause any problems. But some people are afraid of them. Other people are afraid of snakes.

Everyone has fears. The urge that is the root of these fears is the desire for self-preservation. Of course, you desire to preserve and protect yourself, but you should also understand your urges in a little greater depth. And as you examine your fears, you will learn that all of them are somehow false. There is no truth or reality to your fears.

To be creative you first have to be emotionally balanced, and to attain balance you have to understand the negative emotions and how they arise. You have to understand how to use self-counseling with them. But unless you have regulated your primitive fountains, your therapy will not work. In saying this, I am being blunt, and perhaps I am disappointing or offending you by saying this, but it is true. I am not saying that you should not do sex, nor am I telling you not to eat or sleep.

I am merely telling you to begin to regulate the time at which you do these acts. You also have to cultivate and understand your positive emotions and then learn how to express them through your mind, action, and speech. This is the beginning of learning to work creatively with your emotional nature.

Often people ask how long it will take for them to be liberated, and I answer, "One second!" The whole world could be liberated and happy in one day's time, if all human beings used their emotions in a positive way. So learn to work with yourself. All your actions are controlled by your thoughts, and all your thoughts are controlled by your emotions. By comparison with your emotions, thought has little power; if you can use your emotional power constructively, you can channel it. Then your emotional power can be utilized in a creative way and lead you to a height that will give you real happiness.

Chapter 5

MEMORY AND THE NATURE OF MIND

You were taught that Jesus was a great man, that he was a son of God. According to the Vedantic analysis, this is true. Moses, too, was a son of God, as were Buddha, Krishna, Mohammed, and Guru Nanak. They were all born on the earth in exactly the same way that you were born. When they wanted to see, they used their eyes; when they wanted to hear, they used their ears. They walked on the earth exactly like you—so why are they considered to be such great leaders? They were great and powerful because they knew the inner dimensions of life and the laws that motivate them to function. They knew their internal states; they knew their own mind. Like all the great ones, in order to make spiritual progress you first need to understand your own thinking process, and there are many levels to understand.

What do you know about your thinking process? You may try to study the mind through books and external resources, but that is not the way; you need to learn to study the mind without any external help. You need to fully understand the nature of the mind. If you don't understand your thinking process, then you don't understand yourself at all.

However, you cannot really know your mind in its

totality, for a vast part of it remains buried and unknown to you, and is never understood. That is why, in discussing the nature of mind, we often say, "All of the body is in the mind, but not all of the mind is in the body." This means that the mind itself is actually much more vast and expansive than the mere physical body.

But the question of how your body is related to your mind and thinking process is still important to understand. The body, breath, and mind all work together. Your actions are virtually your thoughts, and your thoughts are your desires. Those desires are mingled with your emotions, which arise from the four primitive fountains, or urges: food, sex, sleep, and self-preservation. Thus, the combination of your emotional life and your thinking process is what you call the mind. You perceive things in different ways because you receive them from different angles.

Something exists between yourself and reality, and that is the mind, your thinking process. The mind is a wall between you and reality. But at the same time, it can become a means for you to attain the highest goal in life—to know that dimension of life that is presently unknown to you. You can understand that part of your personality, of which you are presently unaware, by understanding the various functions of your mind and its totality. To deal with this, you have to clearly understand the different functions of the mind.

The mind has two separate compartments: the conscious mind and the unconscious mind. The conscious aspect of the mind is actually very small, but you use and cultivate only this small part during your waking state. The unconscious level of the mind that dreams and sleeps is not under your control, and you do not know much about it. Why do you dream the way that you dream? Why are your pleasant dreams not repeated in the way you would like? Why do nightmares that you don't want appear in your dreams?

Even if you are very learned, or a genius, or a great artist, when you dream you are none of those. When you go to sleep, no matter what you do with the conscious mind, still a vast part of the mind remains uncultivated, uncultured, unrefined, and untapped. This is the unconscious level of the mind. It is used only by a fortunate few, by the great ones, by people such as Christ, Moses, and the Buddha. These men were enlightened and became great because they came into contact with that power through which they learned to control the hidden part of the mind.

The sages know how to expand the conscious level of mind until nothing remains unconscious for them. They expand the field of the conscious mind and are conscious of that which is unconscious for you. For them, there is no such thing as the past, present, and future. For you, because you have no present awareness, there are only the past and the future. You do not live in the here and now. Your samskaras come forward constantly in your mind and motivate you to perform new actions in the present. When this is not the case, then you are thinking about the future. In meditation, however, the sages say that there is no sense of time. Meditation annihilates time and then you are free and can be here and now. That is why they tell us, "Meditate, meditate, meditate!"

If you consider your deepest nature, you can compare yourself to a wheel. A wheel cannot rotate if it lacks spokes; the spokes allow the wheel to rotate. But the spokes will not rotate if there is no hub, the part that remains still and does not move. The entire wheel rotates because of the hub. But that central something, which does not itself move, somehow allows the entire wheel to move—it creates movement.

Such is the case with human beings: there is something called the individual soul, or the center of consciousness, which is not subject to movement, change, destruction, or death. Like the hub of a wheel, it does not move. That central part of us is eternal. But we are not in touch with this center, and so we are constantly afraid and insecure. We become caught up by our emotions. We hardly ever come into contact with that part of our being that is the center of consciousness, from which consciousness flows in various degrees and grades. The little bit of consciousness that we presently experience is only a dim consciousness.

If you place a light inside many levels of shades or filters, the light seen outside will be dim. But if you take away all the shades, one by one, the light will get brighter as you remove each one. This light is your reality. You are like the unmoving hub within the wheel or the light inside the shades. But you do not identify yourself with the center; you identify yourself with the spokes that move and change.

If we continue the metaphor of the wheel, you need to understand that it has four main spokes. They are the four different functions of the mind: manas, the sensory/motor mind and the thinking function; ahamkara, the ego; chitta, the storehouse of all knowledge, through which you receive knowledge; and buddhi, the counselor within you, and that which decides.

Manas is that which you call "mind," but it is merely one aspect of your thinking process. It raises questions such as, "Shall I do this or not?" Whenever you consider doing something, suddenly a questioning comes into your mind and you wonder, "Shall I do it or not? Shall I go this way or that way? Which is more useful? Shall I sit here or there? Shall I speak to you or not?" There is always a doubting nature to your mind, and that is the result of the faculty of manas. This constant doubt is called *sankalpa vikalpa*.

Manas is the only power in you that works both within and without. Its function is dual. Manas is a powerful faculty; it will take in anything from outside, and it will take things from inside outside. It is an importer and exporter. To do that, it employs the ten senses. Manas begins to work the moment you wake up: You picture a cup of tea, so your hand moves, you walk toward the kitchen, and you start to make tea.

Manas, however, is limited. It has no power to make decisions. The faculty that decides is buddhi, the faculty of discrimination. You are usually controlled by manas because you do not take the advice of buddhi, the higher function. But to function well, you need to coordinate the functioning of manas and buddhi.

Buddhi has three qualities: it knows how to judge; it knows how to discriminate; and it knows how to decide. Discrimination means the power, or ability, to distinguish between things (this is a man and this is a woman) and to make a judgment (this is good and this is bad). The deciding quality of buddhi is also important. When you have not learned to decide matters on time, you miss an opportunity. And when you miss an opportunity you regret it and blame yourself; once the opportunity has passed, you finally decide and wish you had taken action. That makes you miserable.

There is a third faculty of mind called chitta, the function through which you acquire knowledge. Chitta is the reservoir of knowledge and memory, of merits and demerits. It contains the power of becoming from within, as well as the accumulation of knowledge from without. Chitta is the intuitive library within you.

There is also a fourth faculty, ahamkara, or the sense of I-ness. You may think that when you go to church you pray to God, but really you are praying to your ego, because every time you pray, you ask, "God, give me this, give me that." This means your "I"-sense is very pronounced—"I" need this, "I" need that. Your "I" is everything to you. God is only secondary to your ego.

Watch how you speak all day and observe which word you use the most—it's the word "I." You have been thinking about

"I" from your childhood on, so that your concept of "I" has become so strong that it has forgotten its proprietor, its real owner, the place from which the knowledge comes. It is atman, the center of consciousness, that appointed this sense of "I" to its position, but the ego has forgotten its role. The ego says, "This body is mine, this home is mine, this wife is mine, these children are mine." All this thinking of "mine and thine" comes from the ego.

The ego creates a serious problem. Your ego is that which has separated you from the whole. It builds a boundary around you, and makes you petty and selfish, and you don't want to share with anyone. The more egotistical and the more egocentric you are, the more you do not communicate with or relate well to others. The ego is definitely helpful in many areas, providing you understand its intended role, but you have completely forgotten this role. You are feeding your ego all the time by saying, "I need this; I want that." During the whole day, only "I" is important, and all other things become secondary. Observe how much you feed your ego.

The lower faculties of mind, manas and ahamkara, are the two troublemakers. Your manas disturbs you with doubts and questions, and your ahamkara separates you from your center of consciousness. But this is due to your mental habits. So you must train both your manas and your ahamkara, and that process is what we call "polishing" your mind. If you lead your ahamkara toward chitta, and train your manas toward buddhi, then you have accomplished something.

Don't do anything in life unless your buddhi, the counselor within, tells you to do it. You need to make internal experiments with yourself: You need to train your buddhi to give a correct, clear judgment to your manas. You also have to train your manas to take the advice of buddhi even though sometimes you don't want to.

Sometimes you become obstinate. Although your buddhi

gives you guidance, you don't want to follow it. For example, if you are lying in bed early in the morning, and your buddhi knows that this is not the time to remain in bed yet you don't get up, you are forming a bad habit. You know that each day you have to eat breakfast and go to the office, and that it takes some time for you to get there, but you don't get up on time. You are awake but you don't leave your bed. This is because there is a coloring of *tamas*, laziness or inertia, in your personality. Slowly you are forming the negative habit of inertia.

The first thing that we teach apprentice swamis or serious students of meditation when they want to develop their mind is that when they wake up, they should immediately get out of bed. The number of minutes that it takes for you to get out of bed will tell you how lazy you are. Your mind will say, "Oh, it's Sunday, I don't have to work, let me stay in bed." That's a bad way of training yourself; it's a bad way of teaching your mind. Regardless of whether it's Sunday or Monday, you should get up and get out of bed. If you remain inert in bed, you are wasting time and energy, and at the same time you are forming a bad habit that affects you on both the physical and mental levels.

So if you really want to discipline yourself and your mind and develop yourself, then the first thing that you have to learn is to get out of bed the moment you wake up, and not remain in bed tossing or turning. Rise, wash, and finish your morning ablutions—and then do something useful. Do not remain idle and inert. You also have to train yourself not to be the victim of sloth or inertia due to overeating or eating foods that create lethargy. Lethargy and sloth also result from not doing things on time, not forming habits which are helpful to you, or not having control over your appetites. Training the physical habits in this way has a direct result in training the mind.

This is an important secret of life: if you remain idle without doing something useful, your mind thinks scattered and random thoughts, and wastes its energy. A thought is like an unripened fruit that is not yet eaten by anyone. Ripening the fruit means bringing a positive thought into action. Many good thoughts die because they are not brought into action, so your good thoughts should definitely be brought into action. Those who are great, successful, creative, and dynamic know how to bring all their good and creative thoughts into action, and how to give a shape and form to their creative thinking process.

To be creative in this manner is a technique that you have to learn for yourself by forming good, sound, healthy habits, physically and mentally. Positive, dynamic people conduct their duties well because they have established coordination between their thoughts, speech, and action. So you need to discipline yourself; do not be afraid of the word "discipline," because to make progress you need to train yourself. Through such training and self-discipline you can truly understand yourself. And when you apply all your resources, intelligence, and understanding to exploring your interior self—the modifications of your mind and your internal states—it will be a fascinating experience.

Your habit patterns weave your character; your character composes your personality, and that's who you are. The Vedanta philosophy says that ultimately we are self-illumined, but that's not the level of yourself that I am describing here. You have a personality, and the personality has a particular character that is woven by certain habit patterns. You are responsible for your habit patterns (although your family has also contributed to them through the way they brought you up and treated you in your childhood).

In this kind of training, books can't help you; nothing external will help you. You have to understand yourself. You need to ask yourself how you think, why you are emotional, and what the problems are with your mind. You need to question why you become emotionally disorganized, why you forget things, and why you do not attend to things properly. You need to consider why you often do not do what you really want to do. Put these questions to yourself, and you'll find the answers.

There is a word in Sanskrit, *apta,* which means "that man who has established perfect control and equilibrium within himself." His actions are consistent with his speech; his thinking process is always coordinated. By contrast, most people start to go in one direction when they actually need to go in the other, and then they suddenly realize that they are headed the wrong way. This is because you have never trained yourself to concentrate and focus. All the world's educational systems cannot help you if you do not educate yourself, but sometimes this becomes difficult. It becomes harder late in life, and, as the saying goes, it's difficult to teach new tricks to an old dog.

Developing the memory is the art of effectively recalling things when you want to. Memory is one of the most important functions of the mind, and working to improve it is part of the process of learning to use all your potentials effectively. You can benefit greatly from the skillful use of memory, from learning how to retain information. Developing a good memory means that when you want to recall something that you know, the mind will come to your aid. A good memory allows your knowledge to be recalled without any hindrance or interference.

Presently, however, your memory is blocked. You have so much knowledge within, but it doesn't come to your aid when you need it. You know many things, but when you need to recall something, that knowledge doesn't help you. For example, perhaps you need the keys to a cabinet. You are searching for them frantically and yelling at your children and fighting with your husband. You yell at him, "Help me find the keys!" And then you scold your children, "You have hidden the keys somewhere!" But actually you discover that you are holding the keys in your own hand. All these actions are caused by your disorganized mind, and that is why this kind of situation occurs. To understand this type of forgetting, you need to consider how you perceive things: When you see something in the external world, whatever you see is received by the optic nerve; then that impression is taken to the conscious mind, and then it is carried to the unconscious mind—that vast reservoir of impressions, samskaras, and memories. Your memory is blocked because you have too many things to do and you cannot handle them. And when the passages between the conscious mind and the unconscious mind are blocked, it is because you do not know how to handle the rush of thoughts and information coming into your conscious mind.

If you learn to pay attention you will not forget things. When you say that you have forgotten something important, it means that you have never really paid attention to whatever you have forgotten. It is stored in chitta, but you did not pay attention to the situation that created it. Attention and memory come from interest. If you have an interest in something, then you never forget it. You have an interest in your home, so no matter how crazy you become or how confused you get, your feet will eventually lead you home. You don't forget your wife or children or your bank because you have an interest in them. So when you realize that you need to search for your keys, the question is, why and how did you forget them? When this happens either you do not understand your thinking process, or you have not paid attention to the things you should.

Thus, memory really indicates and reflects your interest. When you are interested in some topic, you study a book with full attention. If you are not interested in studying a subject, then it becomes difficult for you and you cannot easily understand it. This skill depends on how you train yourself. If children are trained systematically from the very beginning, they don't become absentminded. Being absentminded means that you want to remember something that you don't remember. The desire is there, the fire is there, but you are not really giving fuel to the fire: you don't really have a full interest in what you are doing.

There are some simple, easy exercises that can help you to coordinate and utilize your mind. If you include another five minutes in your daily practice and devote this time to training your memory, they will help you a great deal. But to develop your mind and your memory, you should first understand that whatever you do, you should learn to take a real interest in it. Doing things without genuine interest weakens and dissipates the mind and creates internal conflict.

To develop your memory you should learn to relax yourself consciously for a few minutes every day. Relaxing by sleeping is not enough; it's much more important to learn to consciously relax. So pay attention to relaxing the muscles, the nervous system, and the mind. Sleep can be a great medicine, a great remedy, and a great help when you are fatigued; when you cannot relax yourself consciously, then dreaming can sometimes help you (dreams are the expressions of those suppressions that you have stored during your conscious waking life). Certainly, sleep relaxes you, but it does not relax your total being. Many times you wake up after eight hours of sleep, and yet you still feel tired. There is only one way to fully relax, and that is to consciously relax the body when you are in the waking state. Conscious relaxation should be a part of your daily life. So learn to relax and to reject and let go of the things that hurt you.

Let us say that you have learned to calm the conscious mind by not allowing it to run away to the external world through the agents called the senses. You gently close your eyes and create an atmosphere that is quiet: you don't hear sounds, you don't touch anything, you don't smell anything. Then another problem arises: the mind itself is not relaxed. All the thought patterns that you have stored in the unconscious mind come forward into consciousness. Perhaps you have forgotten to do something, and then remember that you have not done it, so your mind becomes tense. A relaxed mind is a mind that is not preoccupied or disturbed; it is a mind that remains undisturbed.

The following exercise is not a meditation exercise. It is used to improve the memory. It will definitely help you if you do it, but most people will not do it, or if they do it at all, they stop doing it before they allow it to have its effect. But this is a helpful and powerful exercise if you do it systematically. It can actually expand your retentive capacity. There was a time in my life when I thought that I had started to lose my memory, so I was taught this exercise—and now my memory is perfect. I never teach or recommend exercises that I have not personally done. I teach only what I do and what I have done. I have done this exercise and it has helped me.

To begin, sit in a comfortable and steady posture. A steady posture is one that puts your head, neck, and trunk in a straight line. But often it's difficult for Westerners to sit comfortably in a posture on the floor because they have not been trained to do so. Some sitting postures may seem to be comfortable at first, but may actually create pain or discomfort later on. So if you cannot sit comfortably on the floor, don't force yourself to do so and then suffer from a pulled muscle. You can sit on a straight-backed chair with your head, neck, and trunk erect. This is a posture called the "friendship pose," which is described in the Buddhist system of meditation.

Sit quietly. Allow your body to become still, and breathe deeply. Breathing evenly and deeply is the one real remedy for all stress, strain, and fatigue. Deep, even breathing means that when you exhale, you allow the abdominal muscles to push in. This forces the diaphragm to move up and helps exhale the used-up gases. Then, when you inhale, you allow the abdominal muscles to move out, and the diaphragm moves down, creating more space so that you can fill the lungs completely. This exercise is called diaphragmatic breathing.

Diaphragmatic breathing is your birthright. Infants breathe diaphragmatically, but because of your hectic life and the way you sleep, eat, drink, and act, the free movement of your diaphragm has been upset. This has become a habit, so you need to return to your original pattern. Allowing the diaphragm to move with the help of the abdominal muscles is a great factor in relaxation, and learning to breathe in this way is a great benefit. This is how you should breathe all the time.

The next important point has to do with concentration and your mind's focus. There are millions of forms and images in the mind, and your mind becomes confused, and that creates agitation. You are trying to concentrate on a particular form, but many other forms and images disturb your mind. So you need to direct your mind and focus it. We will use a digital system here.

Begin by counting from one to a hundred without saying the numbers out loud. You should count at the speed of one digit a second. The next step is to then count backward from one hundred to one. You will find that it is easy for you to count up to a hundred. But when you count backward from one hundred, you may only be able to go to seventy-seven or so before you become lost, because your mind has never been trained to attend to a difficult task.

Thus, you first count from one to a hundred, and then backward from one hundred to one. There will probably be interruptions. You need to note the interruptions and the kind of interruptions that take place; they tell you about your mental suppressions or procrastinations. For example, if you have told your wife you will do something but you have not done it, then when you do this exercise that interruption will remind you. It is important to observe those interruptions.

When you are relaxed, your mental preoccupations come and distract you, so I encourage you not to have many preoccupations. Don't allow your mind to become congested because whenever you relax, these preoccupations will interrupt your concentration. They interrupt your sleep and do not allow you to rest. Your mind is preoccupied with the duties that you have assumed (you assume duties, and each duty becomes a requirement once you have assumed it).

Learn to keep your mind free for at least a few minutes without interruption, distraction, or interference. If you have never asked your mind to do this, at first it may be difficult, but your mind will learn to follow your bidding. When you ask your hand to pick up a cup and bring it to your lips, it does so. You should learn to direct your mind in other ways as well. It will help you immensely.

As you learn to do this exercise, you are learning to lead the power of the mind—your thinking process and concentration—to follow a particular system, in a particular order. Thus far, the mind has never accepted any order. The mind does not want to do so, but you need to teach the mind to become orderly and organized.

You can start training your mind in this way by counting from one to one hundred and from one hundred back to one, and note how many times your mind becomes disturbed while you lead your mind through this exercise. Notice also the type of interruptions that occurred, and observe the qualities of those disturbances. Consider the origins of these disturbances. In this way you will learn many things about yourself. You should do this counting exercise for at least two minutes every day to retain the power of your memory. It should eventually be extended so that you count up to a thousand and then back. It doesn't take much time—perhaps only ten or fifteen minutes—and when you can do that without interruption, you'll find that your mind has become sharp. There is no doubt about the effect of this exercise.

Sometimes memory losses are due to a lack of routine in your life, or the way you eat. Eating healthy food is important. Doing the headstand can also be beneficial in developing your memory. However, if you decide to do the headstand, you should be careful not to injure your neck. You should do the headstand only as you are taught by a qualified teacher.

Many people are afraid to do the headstand. Fear of doing the headstand means that there is a great fear lurking in your heart. Symbolically, standing on the head means learning to stand on your own feet and having complete control and confidence in yourself. When those who cannot do the headstand ask about it, I tell them to begin by closing their eyes and then to mentally imagine standing on their head. They often say that they imagine themselves falling. They have no confidence in their ability to do such things. You cannot do anything efficiently if you cannot first do it mentally. If you learn to do things efficiently in your mental world, then you'll also be able to do things physically.

There are other exercises for the memory as well. In the chakra system you may meditate or focus your mind on a particular point. For example, you may focus your mind on the space between the two eyebrows, at the pineal gland center. This is visualized as a small circle. The mind never wants to be focused; it wants to move about here and there. The ancient yogis knew that the mind resists being confined in a circle, so their technique was to bring it back to this circle again and again. In the representations of the chakras there are also triangles, which are geometrical and mathematical figures that train the mind. If you carefully observe the process, you will understand why either a geometrical figure or the digital counting system is used to do this. A serious student must learn to direct that great force of the mind in a specific way. If you have not paid this price and have not disciplined the mind in one way or another, if you allow the mind to roam and wander wherever it wants, you'll never achieve much in your meditative training. Working to train and discipline the mind with such simple exercises can definitely improve your memory and concentration.

There is a time in every great man's life—a test from Providence—when he is not understood by others and may be persecuted. You may recall many examples of how great men have remained calm during these times. Socrates is one such example. When he was jailed by the authorities, his students tried to arrange a plan for his escape. But Socrates refused, because he knew that was not a good example for others. Instead, he allowed himself to be persecuted. At the end, he joked when the cup of hemlock was brought to him. He said to the messenger who brought the poison, "Can I give a little share to my *deva*, to the deity who I love, respect, and adore?"

But the messenger did not know what he meant and said, "No, it is meant only for you. You cannot share it with your deity."

So Socrates smiled and drank the hemlock, but before he died he said, "No poison can kill the soul."

Very few people are aware of the soul, which is not subject to change, death, or decay. It is a great power within you. Your mind is very powerful. There is nothing greater except the individual soul, the center of consciousness within. The mind is second only to the soul in power because, for its functioning and expression, it has the ability to borrow power from that center of consciousness, the individual soul. So before the light of the body extinguishes, learn to focus all your awareness within. Then you merely leave your shell here.

Chapter 6

DEVELOPING STRENGTH
AND WILLPOWER

There is an important difference between the mind, the brain, and the nervous system. The following analogy will help you understand: the brain is like a light bulb; the nervous system is like a network of wires; and the mind is like the electric current itself. When the electricity functions, current runs through the network of wires if the wires are not broken. And if the light bulb is not broken, it shines when the current passes into it. The reason you do not attain happiness is because you do not know how to coordinate these different entities.

You need to coordinate your mind and your body. In order to make progress in any aspect of life, it is essential to develop your willpower and your inner strength. Often, however, when you decide to develop your willpower, you may resolve to do dramatic things, and this can cause problems for you. If you cannot yet do what you resolve, then you will find that your strength and your willpower are being damaged rather than developed. So if you sincerely want to develop personal strength and willpower, you should first learn to keep yourself open and be an observer of yourself until your willpower has become dynamic. Instead of making dramatic resolutions, simply decide to experiment with observing yourself.

You can try to use a tape recorder and record everything you think. But millions and trillions of thoughts pass through your mind in just half an hour's thinking. If you try to record them all, it will take you a day. One day's thinking will take you a week to record. So you can see that the mind is not easily studied. This is the external way of studying the mind—what modern science is trying to do, and that's why it has not succeeded.

There is another way of observing the mind. It involves doing experiments within that lead you to the deeper levels of your being. This is an entirely different system. In internal research, you don't have any external means to help you; you have to help yourself. You have to understand the mind and how to go about studying it. You have to understand how to be within yourself systematically. Just as you try to form certain systems, codes, and disciplines for research in the external world, so do you also need a method for research in the internal world. For example, if you have an accident or face a threat or extreme adversity, you use your whole knowledge and your whole being. There is something within you that helps you at such times. This means that your mind has a center. And by knowing that center within yourself you can help yourself.

If you want to know how near you are to this reality, watch your fears and you will be able to tell. You are afraid because you fear either losing something that you have, or not being able to gain something that you want. Whenever you have a fear, you can consider these two possibilities: either you are afraid of not gaining something, or you are afraid of losing something. By examining your fears, you can understand yourself and gain freedom from such fears. The more you live under the pressure of fear, the more you hurt yourself.

Freedom from fear is possible if you know your aim in life and know that you have very little time to accomplish it.

Then, you can coordinate all your resources to completing that mission, and no fear will come to you. But if you do not have any aim in life, then you are constantly afraid of losing things that are actually already lost, and you begin to lose your self-confidence. The moment you lose your self-confidence, your mind cannot decide about anything on time. And if you miss doing what you should have done today, and try instead to do it tomorrow, it is not the same. So learn to depend on your inner knowledge.

Your thought power—the power of your mind and its thoughts—is the most important power you have within you. When you think only of yourself and decide that you want to do something no matter what happens, then you are caught by your selfishness, and only misery results. If you develop in yourself thoughts of serving others, helping them, and showing genuine consideration and kindness, then you will find that you are enjoying life.

Why do people like to think about something before they do it? Because the doing itself is not so important; the enjoyment is not in the action. The action itself is only an expression of your enjoyment. The real enjoyment of something lies in your mind and heart alone. Sometimes you think of something soothing, and you enjoy thinking this thought even though the action itself is not taking place then. Sometimes you do what you consider to be the best and most enjoyable of all acts, but you do not fully enjoy it because your mind is somewhere else. So learn to enjoy whatever you do with both mental and physical coordination. This will happen when you create a real and sincere interest for the things that you are doing. All your duties—whether they are smaller or larger, higher or more trivial—should be done with interest and attention.

Those who are married should consider this: a wife and husband may go to bed merely to do something to please the other, without having the real intention to enjoy each other. Perhaps the woman may think that her husband will be happy if she gives him sex, or he may think that he's giving his love to his wife through sex. When this happens, they are both only imitating something. They are not insincere, but at the same time they are not being fully honest with themselves in such a situation. Such an act is not fulfilling; it causes strain within yourself; and such strain may create disturbances such as physical problems. This happens when people do things without real interest, without real love, or without total will— when they simply imitate something.

When you do something selflessly for someone else, you should also enjoy doing it. If you say, "I am doing this selflessly," but your mind is actually somewhere else, then that is not really a selfless act. That is doing something half-heartedly, absentmindedly, and without any true interest. So learn to enjoy things by putting your whole heart and mind into them, and then you will really enjoy them. If doing something strains you, then you should realize that some part of you within—either your body, mind, or heart—does not fully agree, and that is why you are stressed.

What I am trying to make clear is that although we think we can do the actions of our daily life selflessly, they are not really good for our physical and psychological health if true positive interest has not been created. If we do not do things wholeheartedly, we do not enjoy them no matter how much selfless action we try to do.

When you experiment with observing yourself, remember that your resolutions and deeds should not hurt others. If you try to do something for yourself but end up hurting others, that is actually a selfish act. When you do not want to share the fruits of your deeds with others, that is also self-centered. For example, you may be sitting at the breakfast table and simply grab something for yourself and start to eat it, without having any thought for your partner. Just for the sake of experimentation with your self-centeredness, try instead to be a little bit courteous. Try giving food to your partner first. Nothing will happen to diminish you; you will not lose out on anything, and you will not be deprived of food—but you will observe a positive effect in yourself. You'll find that your whole home life changes.

So if you want to strengthen yourself, try to develop consideration for others and see how much you can do for them. You can divide and analyze all your actions and expressions into many types and categories, but once a day you should simply try to do small things for your children, spouse, or friends. If you develop and cultivate in yourself the desire to give to others, and if you do that once a day without any selfishness, you will be surprised to find that you enjoy everything more.

Selfishness is your biggest enemy. Throughout history human beings have been trying to conquer this enemy called selfishness. They cannot completely do this; they have not accomplished it yet. And those few who have really conquered their selfishness have not ever been understood accurately by others. Look at the lives of Jesus and Moses: They did nothing for themselves; everything they did was for others, but how many people really understood them? When they wanted to communicate the most profound teachings of spirituality to people, only a few, out of millions, came to the mountain where this advanced knowledge was being imparted. Slowly you should prepare yourself for this level of teaching. Knowledge will come of itself; all knowledge is already within you.

To learn to know yourself, you need to take a few minutes for yourself every day. Many people think that meditation is the right solution, and I agree, but most people understand only one part of meditation. In meditation, you sit down quietly and repeat your mantra. During that period your mind remains one-pointed, but after that your mind goes back again to its same previous grooves. This is not the full process of meditation; the full process of meditation is a whole-life process. "Meditation" means "to attend." It means paying attention to the whole of life. It should not be a strenuous act; it should not be forced. Your whole life can be one of meditation. From morning until evening you can meditate, either unconsciously or consciously, and if you do that meditation well, it will bring many benefits.

People often ask how they can do this. My method is to ask myself to consider some question that is on my mind. Once, when I was young, my master asked me to consider where I got my questions. When I told him they came from within, he replied, "Then the answers are also there. I can give you the answers another way, but the answers are there." So from wherever the questions come, there are also the answers, and from nowhere else.

I have questions concerning the welfare of my students, because that is my life's work. Just as you are concerned about your job, so am I also concerned about my job—about my students. Those who lack hope are the first whose images come to me; I think first of what is happening to them. But when they come to see me, I am not bothered or disturbed, because if I disturb myself, then I cannot help them. In the same way, if you disturb yourself about a question, you become more helpless. Your question remains a question because you cannot withdraw yourself from the conflict, like a second person, and watch from a distance. Instead, you identify with everything.

For example, perhaps someone is a very quiet person, and I think she could become a good teacher. Perhaps this question comes to me: "What shall I do with her? What shall I tell her?" When such questions come to me, I say to them,

"Okay, come." I do not push them away by repeating my mantra. What you do, when such thoughts come, is to try to think of your mantra, and this means you are trying to use your mantra to avoid and escape from certain situations, but when you have done your mantra for awhile, your mind again goes back to the same worry. That is not helpful. Instead, let everything come before you for a decision—just watch.

Early in the morning, right after I get up, I go to the bathroom and prepare for meditation, and then I sit down. This is the calmest period of the day, when my mind is quiet. Everyone's mind remains calm at this time, because at that hour the mind is not so external in its focus. I ask my mind what I have to do, and then I set up a dialogue with myself. You should learn to have such a dialogue with yourself. Sit down quietly and ask yourself, "What do I want?"

When you do this, you will find that there are two types of desires: the simple daily wants, and the higher desires. The two types of desires are mingled together. When you sit down to meditate, you think, "I need this thing; I need that thing; I want a good car; my car is old." These are mundane things, but do not allow yourself to suppress these desires by reacting: "Oh, what am I thinking? I should not think like that!" That is not helpful; instead, let the thoughts come before you, and become an observer. Start observing your own mind. Do not try to escape; do not be afraid of your thinking, no matter what kind of thought arises.

What happens to most people is that some thought that comes into their mind disturbs their whole being. Then another thought comes, and that also disturbs them, and this happens continuously. Then they become weak and spineless because of such thoughts. They are afraid because these thoughts keep coming into their mind. This may happen to you. Thoughts that were hidden or unconscious are no longer hidden and come to your attention. You react to them emotionally, and they disturb you. You suddenly realize that a thought exists; you get upset; and then you ask yourself, "Why am I thinking like this?"

The way to work with intruding thoughts is to let each one come, whether it is good or bad. Simply decide that whatever comes, you will not be disturbed. Realize that this thought, whatever it is, cannot disturb your whole life. To think otherwise means that you believe you are weak and that the thought is powerful.

Instead, observe your past. Just watch. Perhaps there was once a day in your past when you were in danger; you were worried or broke, and there was no one to help you. What happened to that time? It is gone. Now you are here. Time is the most powerful filter. You are not the same person that you were twenty years ago; you are growing. Life is a process of growth, whether you want to grow or not. So please prepare yourself for that growth so that it becomes comfortable for you. If you do not prepare yourself, then you remain in a state of stress. Yet sometimes you have to experience even that. Even the worst experiences in the world can teach you something. But sometimes even the best things cannot teach you, because you are not ready. Your whole life is a process of growth, unfoldment, and enlightenment, but often you do not cooperate with that.

The difference between you and an accomplished swami is that you take things into your heart. A wise person doesn't take negative things into his heart. You could tell a swami, "Hey, Swami, you are a fool," and he would never take it into his heart. But you take everything in. If someone tells you that you are a fool, then you may leave that person and never come back. A swami doesn't take in such negative suggestions from outside, but you are constantly influenced by others because you have not yet established your inner strength. The day that you do, you will no longer be moved by anyone's suggestions. So start working on yourself, and learn to build your own personality.

To establish inner strength, decide that whatever negative thought occurs, or whatever others say, you will not accept it blindly. But at the same time decide that you will observe the thought or suggestion and let it come. One person may tell you that you are going to die tomorrow, and then perhaps another person tells you that you will some day become a powerful man. One person says one thing and the other says another. One thought is flattering to your ego; the other thought is crippling to your willpower. Allow both kinds of thoughts to come. Be conscious of them. Whatever kind of thought comes, a thought is still only a thought. Why should you allow a mere thought to affect you? It will affect you only when you accept it. You can observe these thoughts without accepting them as your own or letting them weaken you.

When we have crazy desires and thoughts and we do not know how to organize them or work with them, then our whole life becomes motivated by those desires and thoughts. That is what we usually call "motivation," but we do not really observe or understand our deeper motivations. When you become accustomed to witnessing certain things in yourself, you may still feel bad, but you do not feel so very bad, and if something good happens, then you do not feel it is so incredibly good. You can develop the habit of being more balanced, of losing your destructive sensitivity and reactivity to both positive and negative things.

Do you remember the story of the Buddha and the angry woman? Such people accept that which is beneficial and enlightening, and they gently reject that which is not helpful. The Buddha did not become angry or disturbed when the woman offered him filth, but his disciple Ananda remained disturbed and angry for many days. The Buddha did not take in either the filth or the angry thought. That is the right attitude.

There is no thought that you can keep in your mind forever. It is not possible: a thought is that which comes into the mind and then goes away. So why should a thought that merely comes and goes determine or influence your life? Simply allow it to leave. Before I practice meditation, I allow all such thoughts, both "good" and "bad," to come into my mind and then to go away. You can control both the negative and positive thoughts that leave negative and positive imprints in your mind in this way. If these thoughts are not fulfilled, they lose their power and die.

Just let your thoughts come and pass. Even if you want to keep a thought in your mind, you cannot do it; another thought will come and push it aside. If you think of your husband, then next you will think of your child. Then you will think of your house, and then about your car. Many thoughts come and go; each thought is pushed away by another. There is a continuous train of thoughts. Simply let them go away.

And here is another thing: when some thoughts come, you begin to think about sleep. When such an experience comes, open your eyes. Do not allow yourself to go to sleep in order to shut things out or avoid things; let everything come. If you close your eyes and sleep, it is not possible for you to observe the thoughts that you have stored, and all those thoughts come forward in the mind later. If one particular thought comes and goes, again and again, and if you do not give it any interest, then it will eventually not continue to come back.

The first lesson in this practice is to simply allow the thoughts to arise and then to go away. The second is to bring back before yourself that which is important. The thoughts that are colored by your interest are those that motivate you to act, and not all thoughts have that power. Not all of your thoughts need external expression, so allow them to arise, decide if they are creative or helpful, and then express those that are useful later. You can easily do this.

Usually, however, something important will come to you, and you either start to worry or start to enjoy your imagination. Both kinds of thoughts are actually the imagination at play. Do not form the habit of merely enjoying your thinking process and indulging in it without bringing it to action; such daydreaming is dangerous. Many people do that; they enjoy and indulge in their imagination, but that is not the same as creative imagination. Creative imagination is that process by which you imagine something, and then when it is helpful you allow it to be expressed through your actions.

In my meditation practice, when all the thoughts have gone through the mind, then I start to remember my mantra. You often try to remember your mantra from the very beginning, but there are thoughts waiting for your consultation and you do not pay attention to them. So the thoughts are coming and going in your mind while you are trying to repeat your mantra, and the more the thoughts come, the more you repeat your mantra. The result is an inner battle. That is not helpful; you need not do that. If you use my technique regularly and faithfully, and apply it sincerely, you will be able to really enjoy your meditation.

Meditation is important. But preparation for meditation, the cultivation of an attitude of readiness for meditation, for an awareness of what you should do after meditation, and an understanding of how you should continue this meditation during the whole day, are also important. You need to put this teaching into practice in your daily life.

You need to try to understand and control your mind. First, you need to understand what you are doing wrong. Then, you need to create new grooves for your mind so that it does not automatically flow in its old grooves, but begins instead to flow in new grooves. Learn to counsel yourself and have a self-dialogue. Learn to mentally talk to yourself. Sit down and have a dialogue with yourself; ask yourself why you are doing an action. Many times you will say to yourself, "I don't want to do this, but I have been doing it, so now it's a routine." Then you'll understand the process of habit formation. You need to know a practical method of gaining freedom from those weaknesses that you have formed in your childhood, which have become part of your life and are difficult for you to resolve.

There are two ways to work with your mind: the first is to learn to introspect; the other is to go to a therapist. The five most important requirements for therapy are first, honesty; second, selflessness; next, understanding; fourth, the ability to watch your progress; and fifth, the goal of leading the client toward self-reliance. These five conditions are essential to any therapeutic process.

To introspect you must sit down and observe what you are thinking. But actually you already know your weaknesses and are busy trying to hide them. You cannot face yourself; you don't want to know yourself because you are afraid. A therapist cannot help you unless you stop hiding from yourself.

In therapy, you try to become truthful; both parties must base the therapy on honesty. But unfortunately, that doesn't always happen, and that is why therapy does not always help. Sometimes you hear of someone who has seen a therapist for fifteen years, but nothing is happening. Sometimes patients become so dependent on their therapists that they will not move or make decisions without them. That level of dependence hurts you.

But even if you think that you need a therapist, you cannot see a counselor or therapist every day to solve your problems. Instead, you can learn to counsel yourself. This is the real aim of spiritual teachers. Teachers who know how to counsel within can first help themselves, and thus, by helping themselves, they can also help others. In this system, both the disciple and the master have loyalty and honesty; their relationship has nothing to do with anything worldly. Whatever wealth or wisdom the spiritual teacher has, he will give it to his disciples. That is why great people say, "The burden of wisdom and truth is the heaviest. No one can carry it." The teacher has to hand it over to somebody. He has to give it to his students.

You may have heard the phrase, "When the student is ready, the teacher appears." There are many sages roaming the world who are carrying the truth. They want to pass it on, but they don't find students who are ready. Fortunate are those who are enlightened, and most fortunate are those who are prepared to receive the teachings. A dialogue between teacher and student is called *upanishad.* One wants to learn, and the other wants to teach, and both are dedicated. A special kind of loyalty and sincerity exists between them.

The same principle applies to some degree to therapists and patients. But sometimes the therapist is not completely honest because he needs the income, and the patient is not completely honest because he doesn't want to expose his weaknesses. So that kind of dialogue doesn't always function as effectively as a sincere dialogue between spiritual teacher and student.

And there is something else that you should understand: the spiritual teacher in the external world has a responsibility, but that responsibility is over when he leads his student to the path of silence from which everyone receives knowledge. So depending too much on a therapist or a teacher is not a good thing either. They exist to help you become healthy, happy, and self-reliant. If this is not happening, then leave your guru or your therapist. Either they are not helping you or you are not following their advice.

The sages say that no matter how large a telescope you have, it has no capacity to see what is within you. All the external resources will fail when you try to apply them to the development of inner wisdom. To attain inner wisdom, you'll have to abandon these external devices and learn instead to come into contact with the truth within. If you become a real student, and if you are committed, and if you have decided that you want to receive knowledge from within, you can eventually enter into a dialogue with your own inner self. The best of all friends is your own self, and if you learn to have an internal dialogue, you'll never be afraid of yourself. You'll also never be afraid of anyone else.

How do you begin to counsel yourself? One important question to ask yourself is, "Is my first thought good or bad—is it clear or clouded?" Sometimes your initial thought is helpful. Sometimes, if you think twice and then do what your second thought suggests, that is better. You need to learn for yourself—is your first thought a guiding thought or not? Or does your second thought guide you more clearly? And does your third thought lead you to confusion or to clarity? This is something you can learn about yourself by observing how your mind operates. Through self-counseling you can learn to know when you should trust the advice of your mind.

Sometimes you should doubt your own doubts. Perhaps you have a doubt about whether someone is good or bad, so you look outside yourself and start to analyze that other person. Instead, examine your own thoughts and ask yourself to doubt your own doubts. Just as you can look at others with negativity, you can also see another's positive qualities. At present, you are in doubt and you see both their negative and positive qualities. Which kind of perception and mental attitude do you want to promote in yourself—the divine in you (which manifests as love), the human in you, or the animal in you? Which do you want to promote?

Always be honest with yourself and others. When you lie and then condemn yourself, you lose your willpower, your power of determination. In doing so, you hurt yourself. If you

lie to other people, they will tell you, but if you are lying to
yourself, then nobody can help you. Even good people can do
that; even very good people, gentle people who have been
helpful and loving to others, may constantly lie to
themselves. To avoid this, you have to understand all the
levels within yourself.

To understand your unconscious mind, you have to be
alert and observant and work with yourself gradually. Do not
be harsh with yourself. The mind is like a river; you cannot
stop its thinking. If you try to create a kind of dam or reservoir
in it for some time, like a beaver trying to stop the flow of the
river, eventually there will be a great disaster. So do not try to
stop or suppress your thinking. That's a bad way to try to
understand or control your mind.

You really do not have any innate problems. The problems
that you face today are not created by anybody outside yourself.
If you analyze whatever problem you have, you will realize that
you yourself have created it—and then you confuse others and
create problems for them as well. This means that you create
problems for yourself through your relationships.

If you want to solve your problems in life, you need to
learn to adjust in your relationships. The whole secret of
learning is not to fight yourself, but to simply allow yourself to
know. And here is another secret: The real test of your
strength is when you are tested in the world of your
relationships. The more you isolate yourself, the more you
contract your personality. The more you expand selflessly, and
with an interest in others' welfare, the more you enjoy life.

The saying that charity begins at home means you should
learn to work with your relationships in the miniature world.
The family is a miniature world, and you are testing your
capacity in that miniature world; that is your first training
ground. Then, slowly, you expand your world from your
family to your neighborhood, to your town, to your state, to

your country—and finally to the center within which supplies vitality to the whole of humanity. You will have many opportunities in life to do this. So start to work with yourself. Do not waste energy observing what others are doing. Appreciate what they are doing, and do not condemn or criticize what they are not doing.

You should not isolate yourself. The thought, "I am going to enlighten myself," should not make you egotistical. If you want to enlighten yourself, withdrawing from the world is not life's purpose. Your life's purpose is to live in the world and yet remain above it—and that is possible.

A friend I studied with at the university once saw how happy I was as a swami, and so he also renounced his home and became a swami. In a way he was jealous of me. He looked at me and thought, "What a happy man he is! He has renounced everything and now he seems so carefree and happy!" So he renounced his family and left his home. One day, after three or four years, we met again. We both stayed in the same cave that night. It was winter. We collected some wood and made a fire, and I said to him, "Let's meditate now." But he said sadly, "I cannot meditate. All I can do is remember my beautiful home."

It is important to realize that renouncing things will not help you. Action will help, but not renunciation. If you know how to do your work skillfully, it will help you to make spiritual progress, but if you renounce something because you are afraid of it, or because you are no good at it, then that renunciation is not helpful. It may even create further trouble for you because you will still remember what you have "given up."

You do not have to ignore your duties to become enlightened; you do not need to change your external circumstances. What you really need is to transform your personality. You need to transform yourself, from morning until evening, without disturbing your duties. If you sit down quietly for meditation but ignore your duties, you may actually hurt someone. Students who are not skilled on the path often annoy or hurt others. This is an ego problem.

The question is, how tolerant and gentle are you with others? The more you start to become enlightened, the more gentle you are. Then all things are shown to you, and all things will be known by you through your gentleness. Such gentleness is not a weakness; it is the greatest strength, for love is the strongest thing that you have. Tolerance, kindness, forgiveness, and love—these four make up what we call gentleness. If you are gentle, then you are very strong.

So how do you work with yourself without neglecting your duties? You should develop thirty goals for thirty days, and pick one goal for each day. Practice this yourself; it is a simple thing. These should be small goals, but things you work on steadily. For example, you may decide that today you are not going to lie. That does not mean that you will redouble your lies tomorrow, but rather, that today your whole thinking process is about this: that you are not going to lie. You never claim that you will be able to speak the total truth, you simply decide that you are not going to consciously lie.

When you decide, "I will not lie," suddenly many occasions will present themselves when you could lie. This happens because you are trying to conquer your nature, the part of your nature that you have built unconsciously for a long time. And all your actions in life have unconscious results. It is as if you are digging a hole and therefore making a heap of dirt somewhere else. And suddenly, when you stop digging the hole, you discover that you have created both a heap and a hole.

Then the next day you may resolve, "I will not be unkind to anyone," and as soon as you decide to do that, everything challenging will come to you. The day that you resolve, "I will love everyone and not hate anyone today," you will find that all your enemies are coming to you. They come via telephone calls or letters—or you may hear someone talking about you. Once, when I was young, this happened to me and I became very upset. Someone had written something nasty to me, and my master noticed and asked me what had happened. He used to tell me I was like mercury, so he called me "Thermometer." He said, "Thermometer, what has happened?"

I said, "Look at this nasty letter."

He replied, "Do you want to become more nasty yourself by replying to it in a nasty way? That is not the way to deal with it; read that letter six times, and eventually you will not find anything nasty in it." And that happened. I read, reread, and reread the letter again. My master told me not to reply to it immediately, so I waited, and then six days later I replied to it calmly.

If you adopt thirty points to work on for thirty days, mark them on your calendar and do not tell anyone what you are doing. Just watch the calendar and see what you have accomplished in thirty days' time. The point is not whether you have lied or not lied: it is that you have built your willpower. This is the real process of building willpower. After thirty days you will conclude, "Yes, I have done what I wanted to do." But do not choose big principles that you cannot fulfill—that is destructive. Instead, select little things.

For example, if you decide that for one day you will speak very little—only that which is accurate, purposeful, and non-hurting—you may continue to talk to people, but in setting this goal you will be building your willpower. After you develop willpower, you will have greater self-confidence. And when you have greater self-confidence, you can do anything!

You should never surrender to your own negative habits. You should go on fighting this battle and continue it your whole life. This is not a one-day battle. The day that you accept defeat in working with yourself is the day you are really gone from the platform of life.

Don't accept the idea that you are bad or weak or incomplete. You are a human being. This imposition of the idea that you are bad or good is due to your habits. Do not accept defeat from either adversity outside yourself or from your own negative thinking—go on, and you will overcome it. You can achieve that through willpower; you have that willpower. The more one-pointed your mind becomes, the more concentrated the mind is, and the more dynamic your willpower will become. The more you act selflessly, the more inner strength you will develop. And when you have inner strength you will become free of physical pain. The body may experience pain, but you will not feel it, and the time will come when you will not be affected when the garment of the body is snatched from you.

So learn to be strong. Learn to have strength from the real source of all strength within. Willpower is essential for self-confidence. You should not be overconfident, but you should not lack confidence. Self-confidence comes after you have observed yourself, watched your capacity, and built your will. That is the way to build real personal strength. Then, you can accomplish anything.

There are four types of grace. The grace of guru, the grace of the scriptures, and the grace of that which is divine are the first three. But these three help you only if you have your own grace. These three depend on your own grace. Now, however, your state of mind is enveloped by dust. If you simply shake off the dust, your mind will be clean, so you should make a sincere effort. Even if you make only a fifty percent effort, then another fifty percent of that power will dawn— and that is grace.

So why are some people "graced" and others not? Because they have made a sincere effort. Why do some human beings go into samadhi? Because when they say, "O Lord, I have honestly done all that I can; there's nothing I can do beyond this, through this body," then immediately grace dawns. When you have made effort with all your strength and willpower, help comes from above. That is the "descending force." When you have used all your own ascending force, then the descending force of grace comes.

The grace of the Divine is light. The sun is there, the moon is there, and all the lights of the world are there. The moment you obtain your own grace, this divine grace is there as well.

Chapter 7

DEVELOPING INTUITION AND THE WISDOM OF BUDDHI

Intuition is the path to inner wisdom. But if you want to understand it, you must first understand the avenues through which you receive knowledge. As I have said, in human beings there are three main avenues to knowledge: through the senses, through instinct, and through intuition.

When you perceive something with the senses, a process called "conceptualization" goes on inside your mind, and you form a mental concept. Then the senses continue to react and to receive and perceive information according to the concept you have already formed. You create concepts, or categories, that then organize other sensory experience. But, unfortunately, the kind of knowledge received through the senses is shallow, superficial, and incomplete.

The second source of knowledge is through your instincts. But human beings do not remain in touch with their instincts in the same way that animals do. All the activities of animals are governed by nature, but not many of the activities of human beings are. Somehow, as humans, we have lost that sensitivity to our instincts. And because we are not sensitive to nature and its subtle functions, we do not remain in touch with instinctive knowledge.

The third avenue, intuition, leads you to real knowledge, eternal knowledge. In the modern world, you have been trained to understand only external knowledge, but that aspect of knowledge is incomplete. Great poets, saints, and sages do not use the ordinary routes to knowledge through the mind and senses. For example, the great poet Tagore often said, "My knowledge is not received through the mind; it's received through a vision." Tagore would first see something within, and that vision would inspire him—and he would then act on that vision.

Usually, you don't see things as they are; you see things only partially rather than in their totality. That's why those great people, the ancient men and women of wisdom, are called "seers." They knew and saw things as they are. They saw and understood things, and then they described them. The ancient seers did not see things bit by bit; they saw things in their totality, as they truly are.

You will not find this level of wisdom through the process of sense perception. If you see something with your senses, you don't actually see it as it is. For example, if you merely change an object's angle, it may look quite different, and if something looks different at different times, then the description or experience of that object is incomplete and partial. And when you describe something differently from time to time, it is difficult for others to understand your concept, and thus their conceptualization may be entirely different from yours.

Knowledge received or imparted through the senses is shallow and imperfect. That is why there is always doubt in your mind: "Am I right in doing this? Have I done this correctly?" You need external confirmation; you need evidence that you have done something accurately, because your sense perception is never totally correct and you cannot be secure in it. Yet in order to receive information from the external world and to function in the world, the poor mind must employ the ten senses. Five of these are the subtle receptive senses: seeing, smelling, touching, tasting, and hearing. The other five are the gross senses, or the active senses: the hands, feet, speech, and the organs of elimination and of generation. These ten senses are employed by your mind. All of its input is filtered by these ten senses. You perform your actions with information from these senses.

You cannot change the nature of the senses. The instant you wake up, your mind employs them because they are there, and they are permanently engaged. It's not possible to avoid this situation. Sometimes you think, "When the wind stops blowing and there is no noise from next door, then I will meditate," but the noise in the external world will always remain. For example, in some villages in India they still draw water from the kind of well in which a wheel is pulled by horses or bulls—and it brings up the water. The wheel makes a noise when it runs. Once a horseman came with his horse and wanted his horse to drink. That horse was thirsty and wanted to drink, but the noise scared the horse, and it would jump about. So the horseman asked the proprietor of the well, "Will you please stop this noise so my horse can drink?" The proprietor replied, "But if this noise stops then the water will also stop."

If you expect the whole world to behave nicely, and think that then you'll be able to meditate, forget it! You'll have to accept the external situation around you as it is. If you live near an airport, you don't notice how many airplanes are flying above, but when you first came there you thought it was too noisy. But there are many homes there, and people live next to the airport, and they don't hear the airplanes land or take off any more. If you learn to train your mind, then you can easily be free from noise pollution. But in order to have clarity of mind, you have to learn to train your mind.

Sages and meditation teachers say that you should

meditate and sharpen your buddhi. Why do they say that, and what is there to sharpen? There is a serious problem here: If you study physics you will learn that all the things in the external world are moving. Everything is actually in motion; you are sitting somewhere and you think you are still, but you are moving. Everything is constantly changing, so how can your perception be totally accurate? When something is constantly moving, then the mind cannot accurately record an event. You cannot stop movement in the external world— that's a fact. You can do only one thing: you can have clarity of mind. And this means establishing an understanding between the major functions of the mind: manas, the sensory/motor mind; buddhi, the intellect; ahamkara, the ego; and chitta, the aspect through which all knowledge flows, your storehouse of memories.

Our knowledge is limited to the mere name and form of the body. And any knowledge that is limited to the aspects of name and form is shallow, because all forms change. When the forms change, then the name also changes. Your whole confusion in this world lies in the fact that your knowledge is limited to forms and names which constantly change. Nobody says to an old man, "You little one, you're so cute," but there was a day when he was such a little baby. Nobody wants to kiss an old man in the same way that he was kissed when he was a child. The form changes, the name changes, and our reaction changes. Once the old man was a child; another day comes, and he is an old man.

These constant changes take many new forms; the forms have new names and the names have new forms. We live in a world of names and forms. Our whole life is governed by names and forms, by this particular form or that particular name. If there is a particular form, we impose a name on that form. But everything changes, because everything in the external world is subject to change, death, and decay.

There is another problem: the mind itself is clouded. A clouded mind cannot be decisive and cannot discriminate between right and wrong. You cannot help the fact that things move in the external world, but you can at least help yourself to develop clarity of mind. And if you develop clarity of mind, then no matter how fast this movement goes on in the external world, it can be recorded by the mind.

Thus, there are three reasons why you cannot record things properly with your mind and senses: one is that your instrumentation—your senses—are themselves not perfect receptors; another is that all things in the external world are fleeting, are changing fast; and third, even if they were perfect, and there was no movement in the external world, the mind itself is clouded, so it cannot record the world clearly.

There was once a man who had all the comforts in the world—a wife and children and a home. His children were grown, so he used to attend *satsanga* (spiritual gatherings) and visit swamis and yogis and listen to their discourses. Everyone talked about enlightenment and what a wonderful place the Himalayas are, so he decided, "Enlightenment is the only thing worth seeking in life."

So he told his wife, "Look, I am old now, I'm eighty. You've been a faithful wife and partner to me, and I respect you, and with all my reverence I love you, but I want to be enlightened. Will you give me permission to go? You have the children and everyone to look after you."

She replied, "I give you my permission with one condition: when you have realized something, will you come back and let me know?"

He said, "I faithfully promise it. You are my partner. I would like to impart my experience to you."

Renunciation means you don't ever come home again to claim that this home is still yours or that this wife or children are yours. You have a right to renounce if your wife permits you to, but if she doesn't permit you, then it's not renuncia-tion—it's escaping; it's running away. Renunciation means that you first have something, and then you renounce it. So this man renounced his home and walked away, but his imagination and mind were undisciplined. That night the man thought he saw a ghost on the other side of the road, because such fears still existed in his mind. He had renounced his home, but he had not worked with his fears. He did not have any real knowledge or wisdom. He turned around and began walking back to his home, but then he thought, "I have already renounced my family. What shall I tell my wife and children?"

A man's ego is very strong, so he thought, "What shall I say to my wife? I have renounced." So once again he turned toward the Himalayas, but again he encountered the ghost. Again and again he went back and forth, hoping that eventually, perhaps, the ghost would be gone, but the ghost was always there so he could not pass it. Soon it was four o'clock in the morning. It was still dark, and the ghost was still there. Then he saw a snake on the road behind him, barring his path toward home.

Just then a wise man, who was also traveling on the path, came along and said, "Son, what's the problem?"

The man said, "Sir, I am a renunciate."

The wise man said, "I can see that you have renounced, but I don't think that you have practiced or learned anything! What's really the problem?"

The man replied, "There is a snake on the road behind me, and in front of me there is a ghost."

So the wise man told him to come with him and gave him courage. When they reached the snake the sage told him to kick it, and suddenly the man realized that the snake was only a piece of rope. That illusion had taken place because the man had the habit of perceiving things merely through his senses. But the senses never tell you about things as they are; they will only give you partial knowledge. When he kicked at the piece of rope and knew it was only a piece of rope, he felt foolish. How foolish we are when we use only one avenue of knowledge—the senses—and rely on it totally, and suffer because of it our whole life. There are other avenues to knowledge that we should learn to use.

Then the man said to the sage, "Okay, sir, you helped me with this problem, but how about that problem?" He pointed to the ghost. The wise man told him to follow along, and when they got there, the wise man said, "That is an electric post which looks like a ghost."

Mere renunciation will not make you a sage, especially if your mind remains confused and clouded. Do not forget this: leaving home does not make anyone a sage. Failing to meet your responsibilities does not make you enlightened; escaping from the world does not enlighten you either. So be wherever you are, and enlighten yourself there. You don't have to run away and go here and there. You only have to know the simplest method of working with yourself, working with all the avenues of knowledge. All that you need for perfection and enlightenment is already within you. But you have these three problems: a clouded mind, the limitations of your senses, and the changing nature of the external world. So how can you know things as they are? How can you end this confusion and stop these internal debates when the senses and mind themselves cannot record things accurately?

Unrelated ideas, subjects, and thoughts go on in your mind constantly. You fantasize about reality, and that creates conflict for you. And if you constantly deceive yourself, the day will come when you will no longer have confidence in yourself within. Then you will need someone's advice all the time, even to confirm small things, such as whether there is a piece of bread in your hand. You will lose all your confidence because you are deceiving yourself, and this distorts your mind. You know that what you are saying is not true even though you are trying to say something that is true. And that process disturbs the clarity of your mind.

This is why you have the problems and disagreements that take place at home and elsewhere. For example, no one actually lies; there is no such thing as a lie. Even if you think that you are lying, it's not possible because you yourself know that you are lying. So within yourself, there is no lie. If you try to utter a sentence that is a lie, you cannot really do it. You can say inaccurate things; you could call a table a blackboard, and someone might consider that a lie, but it is actually not a lie. It is merely that you are not relating well or accurately to objects.

No one on the earth can truly lie. If someone says something that seems untrue to you, it may be because that person is seeing something from a different angle. If you say, "Swami Rama is God," this is inaccurate; those are unrelated objects. You are not relating God and little Swami Rama properly. And when you do not relate things well mentally, then you hurt your imagination. You are trying to "tease" your imagination, and teasing your imagination will rob the purity of your mind. We are already confused enough, so, as the ancients say, "Don't confuse yourself further by lying."

"Lying" means not relating to things as you see them; it means that you are not reporting things as you see them. But that doesn't actually matter, because from another viewpoint we are already lying for we do not know or see things as they truly are. So no matter how much truth we think we speak, it is equivalent to a lie because we don't yet see things as they are. Our avenues for knowledge, our instrumentation, our "employees," are not functioning according to our ultimate goal. Our eyes want to see the whole, but they cannot; they have limitations. So whatever we say is equivalent to a lie, and yet we will boast that we are speaking the truth.

So what can you do in the external world when everything is subject to change, death, and decay? When the senses are untrained, they will give you distorted input, and that creates constant confusion within. If you accept that there is confusion in your mind, however, and if you understand that, then nothing will lead you astray. But if you don't have that understanding, and if you enjoy that confusion, then your mind will create chaos within, and that confuses you even more. There will be no end to your confusion because of this situation.

When the ancient sages analyzed this problem, they asked the questions, "What should we do with these instruments, our senses? Whatever knowledge we receive, we receive through our senses, so how can we cope with their inaccuracy?" To answer these questions, the sages tried first to understand the nature of their own mind. They found that you should develop clarity of mind, and learn not to be distracted by external confusion or stimulation. But if you have never trained your mind in how to deal with the external world, then there is sure to be confusion. You wonder if the mind is more powerful than the senses. You wonder how many powers of the mind there are, and how they can be understood, controlled, and guided if you understand yourself. The sages say that first you have to understand your mind—called the *antahkarana*, the internal instrument—and then you can think of developing clarity of mind.

The basic nature of the mind is simply to continue to function and to flow all the time. There is a parable in the East about this. Once, a king and queen visited an exhibition, and after seeing many beautiful things for many hours, they noticed a very small, beautifully carved box. The queen admired it more than anything else, and the proprietor said, "The rest of the exhibition is nothing; this box is something truly great. No one has anything better." The king and queen asked why it was so special, and the proprietor opened the box and something like a genie jumped out of it.

"What is so great about this little genie?" the queen asked.

The proprietor said, "Don't call it little, Your Majesty. It's great and powerful! Whatever work you give this genie, it will do it in a second's time."

"We have such a large kingdom," the queen replied. "If we had something like this, we'd be very fortunate!"

So they bought the box, and in their excitement they both started working with the genie as soon as the box arrived at the palace. But that whole night they could not sleep: the moment they gave the genie something to do, it would immediately do that work and then say, "Give me more work or I will eat you up!" They had to keep it constantly occupied, or it would devour them. He continually demanded more work, and they were running out of things to have him do. They did not know how to handle that genie.

Finally, the Prime Minister, the wise man of the country, was called in to resolve the problem. The king told him, "We bought this genie and it is a dangerous creature. It works wonderfully; it has tremendous power, but the moment it finishes its work, it says, 'Give me more work or I will devour you.'"

The Prime Minister told the king and queen that he would solve the problem. Then he turned to the genie and said, "I am the Prime Minister of this country. I want you to go out and get the tallest bamboo tree from the entire forest— the largest and tallest."

The genie got it in a second's time, and then the Prime Minister said, "Dig it into the ground outside," and the genie did that. Then the Prime Minister said, "Whenever their majesties give you work, you do the work; the rest of the time you go up and down this bamboo pole." Thus, by keeping the genie occupied, the king and queen were saved.

The mind is a genie! The great sages say that whenever you have to work, the genie within your mind works, but when you want to stop, it does not allow you to rest. It functions all the time. It does impossible things; it thinks of total impossibilities. It is a magic-maker. The mind is amazing. And if you think that you have imagined something incredible, just wait—someone else's mind is even more fertile and imagines something even better.

Wherever you travel, your mind is there. And sometimes it even goes where you don't travel. Then you realize that you are here, but you aren't really here—you are thinking of going home. But when you are at home, you are thinking of being somewhere else—at work or at a meditation retreat. And the moment you arrive at the retreat, you think of your home, your husband, your children, and your things. You are not ever here. It seems that one of the definitions of mind is "that which is not there, wherever you are!"

To truly understand the mind you have to understand your own thinking process—not only your thoughts, but also your emotions. So how do you actually do it? You have to train one of the aspects of your mind to study the totality of your mind. You have to train a part of the mind, your buddhi, so that all the functions of the mind can be studied through the use of that one part.

Vedanta philosophy says that you first need to understand free thinking, and this will come when you fully understand each part of the whole wheel of the mind separately. Vedanta also says that the mind can be understood in many ways. An entire *sadhana* with many practices is devoted to this process. But even if you know exactly what the mind is, mere knowledge will not give you control over it. Control means knowing the way in which to direct your mind. It does not mean preventing the mind from functioning; it means being aware of the mind and having a choice about the way it is directed. On this path, you yourself are a laboratory for research. Your internal states are the many instruments you have to learn to use in order to understand the consciousness that flows from the center within you. So learn to tap those sources within, those sources of real knowledge—knowledge that can never be challenged, knowledge that is self-evident and pure.

But you are confused because you accept what you see, and you don't check your perceptions. You should doubt everything—even your doubts. Before you take action, you should confirm that what you are thinking is correct. First, doubt and don't take action until you have thought it out and know that you are correct in your perception. If you work with yourself in this way you will learn what kinds of thoughts are accurate and what kinds are confused.

For example, when I was very young, I spent all my time with my master. I learned everything from him. Once, I learned from him what theft means. He never used to keep any money, but one time he knowingly kept five rupees in his pocket and then he created a circumstance in which I needed five rupees. So I put my hand into his pocket and took them out and gave them to the person who needed the rupees.

My master said to me, "Come here. You are a thief!"

I said, "What did I steal?"

He replied, "You took five rupees from my pocket."

I said, "But you're my father!"

He replied, "Of course, but a son can still steal from his father's pocket, and a father can still steal from his son's pocket."

I said, "No, I don't feel that way; that's not stealing."

He answered, "You should try to understand the real definition of things. If you train your determination, decisiveness, and judgment, then you will understand."

Then I said, "What do you mean by stealing? I did it openly, right in front of you."

He replied, "Whether you did it in front of me or not, you robbed me. You may be looking at someone, but if you rob him and go away, that doesn't mean it's a righteous thing to do!"

I said, "I still don't understand."

He told me, "You have to understand this today. Taking someone's things without his permission is theft. Theft is when you take or deprive someone of something without his permission."

And that was the last day I ever did anything like that. I never repeated that action. In your daily life, in developing your moral code, you need to understand the real meaning of things. And this involves training the mind.

You commit thefts from yourself mentally by not allowing your buddhi to function freely. And if you do not allow your instrument to function, it will become rusty. Then, when you want to use it, it will not function well. You are not using the finest instrument that is deep within you—one of the finest instruments that exists—and it has become rusty with disuse. So you have to purify it. When you decide to purify your buddhi, try to remove whatever rust has developed by consciously refining your whole mind, and don't allow any more rust to develop.

In the last analysis, however, the mind cannot be completely understood by the mind itself. There is something beyond mind. This does not mean that it cannot be reached. Beyond does not mean far away or unattainable. This has been wrongly translated. According to Vedantic philosophy and Yoga philosophy, "beyond" means within. Your senses are beyond your body, your mind is beyond your senses, your soul is beyond your mind. Beyond means inside, at a deeper level.

We live on certain levels; we have created certain values for ourselves, and that's how we live. Then we think that is reality, and yes, it's real, because reality is a relative term. But the waking reality is different from the dreaming reality, and the dreaming reality is different from the sleeping reality. But the absolute reality lies beyond. He who knows only how to live in this waking reality, adjusting and reacting to everyone, is a fool. So do not search for that which is beyond on a superficial level. When you become conscious of something within you that is beyond the mind, when you depend on that which is deeper and finer, then instead of depending on the mind, you can understand the mind.

The sages conducted internal study and research on their own minds, and their findings are explained in Vedanta psychology (which describes the mind beautifully). Vedanta psychology says that the mind—the antahkarana, or internal instrument—is like a wheel with many spokes. *Karana* means "a function taking place," and *antah* means "inside"; so *antahkarana* means your "internal functioning," or what is happening within you. That's what modern psychology is trying to understand.

For example, the faculty of manas, the sensory-motor mind, will say, "Do this," and it will immediately add that if you don't do that, something bad will happen. Manas will remind you that if you commit a theft, you'll regret it. It will teach you that if you don't commit a theft, you'll feel like a good person. It will tell you that if you commit a theft you'll become rich, but if you are caught you will go to jail. All these *sankalpa vikalpa*, these thoughts and arguments going back and forth—giving first one side and then another side of the debate—are the function of manas.

Manas asks, "Shall I do it or not?" But if you don't have guidance, if you have not yet learned how to guide this particular part of your mind with buddhi, the intellect, then you cannot make decisions on time. The counselor within you is buddhi, which tells you how to decide, judge, and discriminate. This process is going on inside you all the time, on different dimensions and to different degrees. So whenever you perform any action, ask your buddhi to tell you whether it is right or wrong.

The mind is like a wheel. Manas, buddhi, ahamkara, and chitta are the spokes. And inside, at the deepest level, there is the hub, the center of consciousness. You cannot know the center hub unless you know the wheel. The wheel of the mind rotates because of its spokes, and these spokes rotate because of the hub. The world only inspires or motivates the mind. All power comes from the center. So you should learn to understand your own mind.

No one outside you can give you salvation. I know this will disappoint you, but it is the truth. Christ only enlightened twelve people because the others were not yet ready. He was a great man, and he had such a great personality. He could do wonders. He could change water into wine, but he could not enlighten all the Christians. Moses could not enlighten all the Jews. Krishna could not enlighten all the Hindus. Buddha could not enlighten all the Buddhists. Mohammed could not enlighten all the Muslims. We all have prophets; we all have great religions. But the truth is, we have to enlighten ourselves. You have to light your own lamp; nobody else will give you salvation.

The simple method to enlightenment is to first know yourself. Learn to work with yourself; don't give up on that. Give up on anything else, but don't give up that goal. Remind yourself, "I will continue to work with myself. I can do it, I will do it, and I must do it." Remember these three sentences: "I can do it, I will do it, I must do it."

Whenever anything comes into your mind, ask your buddhi, the counselor within, "Should I do it?" The moment you ask, "Should I do it?" it means you are counseling with your buddhi. It means you are purifying your buddhi. You may commit mistakes once, twice, or even three times, but buddhi will always guide you more and more clearly. Slowly your ego will become aware of the truth. And the day that the ego becomes aware of the truth, the barrier it creates will vanish. The same power that is presently your enemy then becomes your friend—and that is a delightful experience.

Your mind is like a genie. It is higher than any other power; it is faster than the speed of light or electricity; it is the fastest of all entities. Nothing has ever gone beyond that speed except one—and he is an enlightened one. To be enlightened means to have gone beyond the speed of mind. Spirit is beyond the speed of mind. Spirit is everywhere. The poor mind cannot match its speed.

When the mind becomes aware that Spirit is everywhere, then it surrenders. It learns that all the power it has is due to Spirit—the source and the fountainhead of life and light within, the source of consciousness. Then the mind surrenders. You reach such a height that the mind doesn't function any longer. It is still there, but as it becomes aware of the reality, its ego vanishes. That is the meaning of self-surrender. It is the highest of all yogas.

The knowledge of the mind, the senses, and instinctual knowledge do not help in this. They are important, and we need them and can use them, but the highest of all knowledge is intuition. And this comes only when your buddhi is purified and your mind is refined. Intuition does not require any evidence at all; it does not need to ask if something is right. When you have intuition, you don't have to ask about it, because you know it's right. That knowledge helps you see things and know things as they are, and then you no longer see things incompletely and partially. Fortunate are those who receive intuitive knowledge.

From the age of three I've studied with many sages who have devoted their time and their lives to the path of enlightenment. I've thought about these subjects for a long time. I've learned about human beings from these great sages, and through their association, by their grace, all that I have heard is stored in the bed of my unconscious. They taught me that intuitive knowledge is the finest of all knowledge, and I have confirmed this from my own experience. Anyone who is on the path knows it, and I am describing the same teachings to you.

People don't go to expensive bars and drink the best wines from paper cups. The most expensive wines are drunk from a goblet. To experience good wine, you need a good instrument, a good cup. To experience intuitive knowledge, you need a sharp buddhi and a refined mind. Otherwise, they will obstruct the flow of knowledge.

But if you have not worked with yourself, how do you expect that highest knowledge to dawn? If you have not tilled your land, how do you expect the crop to grow? If you want to receive intuitive knowledge, you must remember that no matter how many mistakes you have committed, no matter what you think about yourself or what your friends or neighbors think about you, there is a great library of intuition within you. Deep within you, within the recesses of your being, lies chitta, the library of intuition, but you do not know how to reach it and you don't have access to its wealth. It's as if there is wealth hidden in your own home but you think that you are a pauper.

We all are rich deep within. Great artists, poets, and dynamic people unconsciously receive some of that knowledge, some small fountain from that library within, and that's why they become great. It takes very little for this to happen—just a drop of that richness. And those who receive even a drop start to make poems, or start to paint or begin to sing or dance beautifully—all because of that infinite library within.

That library of intuition within you is chitta. It is the source. When you work with yourself, it will open up for you. A spark comes out of the intuitive library, and that is a hunch. A hunch flashes for a second, and then you cannot call it back. Sometimes it will come like a flood. When you come in touch with that finest of all knowledge, and that highest of knowledge gives you clarity of mind, then your whole life is a poem and a song.

Chapter 8

TRANSCENDING DESIRES AND PURIFYING THE SAMSKARAS

Happiness is the ultimate goal in life. All your actions in this world, whether eating food, getting married, or having children, homes, or friends, are an attempt to find happiness. But do they give you happiness? They offer the best of joys—for a moment—but they do not give you everlasting joy. You find their joy, and then you return again to the same world of conflict, sadness, sorrow, and worry. Human union gives you a joy that is only a glimpse, a foretaste of something higher, which is everlasting.

Consider what you are actually doing: through your actions you are trying to fulfill your desires, one after another. Like crazy people, you repeat the same actions every day, trying to fulfill a desire—and yet it is never fulfilled. Your actions just put more fuel on the fire of your desire. But you cannot live without performing actions. No human being can possibly do that.

For example, perhaps a couple builds a home with a modest budget. Both the wife and husband are happy with the beautiful house. But there is nothing inside because they do not have money for the carpet and furnishings. So now they desire to acquire those things, and soon they develop desire after desire. You have one pillow cover, and now you need two or three more. You need dolls for the children. The children grow, and now they need a pet dog. So on it goes and there is no end to it. You are caught in the snare of desires and you cannot get out of it. Things are meant for you to use, but they are not yours, so don't allow yourself to become attached to them. Things will always disappoint you.

This is the process: You want to fulfill a desire. You have a desire, so naturally the desire will motivate you to fulfill it, and you are doing something to try to fulfill it. But in a few days' time you will discover that your desire is still not fulfilled. So then you go on to another desire. This entire process drives you crazy and creates emotional problems. In this way you make your unconscious mind into a junkyard.

You do this kind of thing unconsciously with all your desires, but such experiments have already been done by the great sages long ago. You should follow their advice: the sages taught that you can never attain anything truly great by fulfilling desires alone. You have to understand this point to make progress. Attaining objects alone can never make you happy. So the question is, how do we attain a state that is free of desire?

You have desires, and you should have desires. You cannot live without having things. But you need to learn a way to live in the world happily, even though you have desires, and there is a way to accomplish that. It is called the path of action, or the path of karma. You can follow this path if you know how to perform your actions with the right mindfulness. But you are not yet happy because you do not know how to attenuate your desires.

You do not need to become swamis, sannyasis, or renunci-ates and renounce all your desires. Renunciation itself is not important; what is important is learning to live in the world, yet remain unaffected by it. No matter who you are, whether you are a swami or an ordinary person, you should learn this technique. It's not easy, but it is not impossible to attain a state that is free from desires. And even while you still have desires, you can be happier if you understand how to reconcile them.

At present you try to fulfill your desires through your actions, but it is not your actions that actually make you unhappy. Doing actions is your birthright. You cannot live without action. So you are caught in a trap: Human beings cannot live without performing actions, but when they perform the action, they have to reap the fruits of their action—that's a certainty. And when they reap the fruits of their actions, then those fruits motivate them to do further actions.

Anything that you do repeatedly for a long time becomes a part of your life, and that is a habit. You all are beautiful from within because the soul is immortal, but your emotional habit patterns have created a mask for you. Whatever you express, whatever you understand, as far as you can go, is made up of your habit patterns. And all your habit patterns depend on the four primitive fountains of emotion.

If you consider an emotional problem, however, understanding one single emotion is not going to help you much. If you say, "I become emotional and angry with my husband. He comes home tired, and I should not do that," you might stop that one behavior, but there is still something at the root of the behavior that you do not understand. Somewhere, there is an imbalance in how you manage your primitive fountains: food, sleep, sex, or self-preservation.

For example, many years ago, "Mama" was the first chairman of the Institute in Chicago; she was a very loving person. We had a wonderful relationship. But she had a bad habit: she was really overweight. I said, "Mama, you should lose weight, you know."

She said, "My diet is fully controlled."

Her sister Kitty said, "At night she eats everything in the refrigerator, but she doesn't remember that in the morning."

Why did she do that? In her sleep, she would go to the refrigerator, eat, and go back to bed, and in the morning she would scold Kitty for eating the food. So one day I sent one of the residents there to discover the real situation. I told her not to say anything, but to simply watch. That night, the girl found Mama going to the refrigerator for pie. So I told the girl to remove all the pies from the refrigerator. The next night, there was no pie when Mama opened the refrigerator door. So she opened her eyes and realized what she had been doing.

Many things that you do, you do unconsciously, although not necessarily in your sleep. You are not aware of what you do or why. When you do something unconsciously, it means that your habit pattern is very deep, and you are not aware of it. When you do things unconsciously it means that you accept a kind of helplessness in that area, and when you accept defeat, that's the worst thing you can do to yourself. When you accept defeat in working with yourself, then you secretly condemn yourself, and then, when someone says something you resent, you become outraged and offended.

In the Christian tradition, Saul was transformed and became Paul because one day he listened to his conscience and understood that the path he was following was not the right path. Then he became a sage. In your case, however, you often knowingly continue to do things that are wrong. You know that one course of action is right, and yet you do not do it. For example, you waste time and energy in useless ways: in gossip, hatred of others, and in animosity or jealousy. This is a sin against your own conscience. When you know that something is right, and yet you go against it, you act against your own conscience, and that weakens you. To act against your own conscience kills the powerful force within you, your determination and willpower. And if you kill your willpower, you can never be dynamic—your dynamic will will depart. You know what is right for you, and yet you often go on repeating wrong action. This is a crime. You know that something is bad for your growth, and yet you constantly repeat it because of your bad habits. So you should learn to understand your own mental habits. This is actually easy; it is not at all difficult.

Remember that habits are controlled by your thoughts, and your thoughts are controlled by your emotions. For example, modern people think that they know many sciences and that they are wise, but inside they are lonely and afraid. Their pockets are full of pills and their homes are dispensaries. They have huge locks on their doors. They are fearful people because there is nothing inside themselves. They have no anchor in life, and their movements are not free.

How can you enjoy such a life? If you live under the pressure of such fear all the time, how is it possible for you to enjoy life? You do not enjoy it and you cannot enjoy it because you are afraid of losing what you have, and not gaining what you desire. These two fears constantly haunt your happiness.

Human beings are afraid because of their human weakness; fear is the result of human ego and ignorance. You are afraid of others because they are different from you. But there is only one reality. All your fears will create problems for you only as long as you separate yourself and isolate yourself from that truth.

To be free from fear means to be one with that truth; once you know that truth, you are free. Then once you know that the person you fear has the same center of consciousness that you have, you are not afraid of that person. The great sages in their forest dwellings have made experiments on the subject of human fear. They say that even ferocious animals, such as tigers and snakes, will not hurt or harm you if you know this truth.

I had this experience once. I was in silence in the mountains and I was very tired. It was about three o'clock in the afternoon, and by nature I get sleepy at three o'clock because I don't sleep at night. So in the daytime, after lunch, I have a habit of taking a nap. This day I still had to climb another four miles, but I got tired at three o'clock. I had already climbed five miles, so I rested, had some food and water for my lunch, and then found a cave and went inside. I was so sleepy that I lay down right there. I had a kind of poncho blanket that I put over myself and soon I was half asleep.

Gradually, I realized that something was crawling over my body and scratching me. Two small tiger cubs were playing and making noise. They thought that I was their mother, and they were scratching, running around, and licking me. My eyelids were very heavy, but this was not a dream. I said to myself, "Oh no, they are tiger cubs! What will happen when their mother comes?" This thought came into my mind, but I was very tired, so I tried to sleep. I could not really sleep in that situation, but I tried to.

This lasted for about half an hour when suddenly I saw a shadow in front of the cave. I opened my eyes and saw a tigress standing there, waiting to come in. I did not have any weapon, so I thought, "I'm not hurting your cubs. I don't have any intention to harm you. If you move aside, I will go out and you can come in." That's exactly what happened: the tigress stood aside, and I went out, and then she went into her cave. There is a simple saying in the *Ramayana* that is true: Even the smallest of creatures and animals understand what is right and what is wrong.

You are all alive, and you want to live for hundreds of years. You do not really believe that you are going to die. Nobody can believe it. You see other people dying, but you don't see yourselves dying. So the fear of death that you acquire is terrifying to you.

Certainly, you should realize that you have a body, and it is a useful instrument so you should keep it healthy. But the body will not lead you to enlightenment. When you raise your identification from the level of the body, then there will be no pain in the body. Don't ever let yourself be terrified by death, for death is merely a part of life. Death is sure to come. It is never painful. That which is painful is thinking about death.

Because we are human, we have to die, so why do we not usually remember that? Actually, both realities exist. We see that people die every day. But a part of us never dies—and we also know that. If we go around preoccupied with the thought, "I will die just as my neighbor died!" then we cannot do anything useful in life, but if we understand the immortality within us, then we will be happy; then there will be no fear. So before the light of the body extinguishes, learn to focus all your awareness within. Then, you merely leave your shell here.

Do not forget that this life is only a journey, and you are a traveler. On this journey, you must have something solid for yourself, like a firm rudder. If you lose your rudder, your boat will float aimlessly and you won't know where it is going. Your rudder in life is to remember that you are on a journey, and that this world is not your home.

When you are on a journey, you travel light; you don't carry everything that you have at home. You take just enough money for the trip. That's the principle: to have enough money means to have inner wisdom; traveling light means not to have any anxieties or burdens in your daily life.

A seeker should think, "I am only a guest here in this world. A guest cannot afford to be rude to the host. What right have I to misbehave or to be greedy? I am on a journey and I must complete my journey." This life is like a crowded procession. You have to see that you don't hurt anyone and that no one hurts you. To achieve that you must learn to be skillful. So learn the skill of performing your actions, yet remaining free from reaping the fruits. That is accomplished when you cultivate the attitude of love.

If I perform an action, I am bound to reap the fruits of the action, and if you do an action, you are also bound to reap the fruits of your action. We are not caught by our actions, but by their fruits. But if I do my actions with love for you, and at the same time, if you do your actions with love for me, then we are both free. Humans have not yet learned this skill. Humanity has not yet learned to do things for others, selflessly and lovingly. That's why the sages say that love liberates, that love is real knowledge. So learn to do things for others, because learning to act in this way liberates you.

Moses remained all alone without food and water on the mountain for many days because he knew that there is something special that human beings have to attain. He was born for that and he had to do it. All the world's great men and women have had this characteristic of selflessness, and all also understood the law of karma, no matter which religion they followed. The Christians say, "As you sow, so shall you reap," and the Buddhists recognize the same truth. Buddhism is built on the foundation of the law of karma. The Hindus, too, believe this principle, and it is found in the Koran as well. There is no "forgiveness" in this law; there is no escape from its consequences. If you have sown the seed of an apple, you won't reap a guava. But the human being is a peculiar creature and says to God, "O Lord, I have sown an apple seed, now please create a guava with it!"

When you learn to do things for others, there are four aspects to the process: you learn to give; you learn to love; you learn to be free; and you learn to follow the law of karma. If you do not follow this process, you cannot ever attenuate your many desires. I have said that all the strains of your negative emotions arise in some fashion from the primitive fountains.

You need to learn to understand these primitive fountains and their effect on you. In order to do that, you need to learn to observe your mind and to counsel yourself. Then, you can be free of the burden and unhappiness you have created by your own desires.

You should allow your good thoughts to be expressed through your actions. But many times your good thoughts are not fully expressed, and in this way you constantly damage and kill that sensitive inner part of you which would help to bring about your own enlightenment and growth. Then a time comes when something negative builds up inside you because you are constantly hurting yourself. This is the greatest of all sins—to kill your conscience.

The conscience is not your mind, your primitive urges, or your emotions. It is the clear mirror within you, and it is helpful in dealing with your mind and its problems. If you do not kill your conscience then you'll never commit mistakes, because your conscience will guide you wisely. But the more mistakes you commit, and the more you blame and condemn yourself, the more you hurt your conscience. So don't allow your conscience to be enveloped by the dust of ignorance, and don't shatter or damage your conscience. Keep it clear by listening to it.

In the Western hemisphere everyone has a job, but no one values it because they think they can easily get another. You are confident about that—if a doctor does not want to practice medicine, he can leave and become a carpenter the next day. But in other countries this cannot happen because they don't have such an open economy as you do, and it's difficult to get jobs. But here, even though you have freedom, everyone is unhappy. You do things which you do not really want to do, and yet you persist in doing them. This creates a constant conflict in your mind, and that conflict is the source of unhappiness.

Your ancestors, the great sages, said to let all your actions become your duties. This happens when you understand that you are really doing the action for another—your wife or child or neighbor or country—or for humanity. Actions become duties because you accept a responsibility to do them. If you think, "This person is my wife, so I should do certain things for her," then any action that you perform with that awareness becomes your duty. Unfortunately, however, I've known housewives who felt burdened by the pressure of their duties, and when I say, "Why don't you sit down and have a cup of tea and relax," they protest.

"I have to go home; I'm married," they say. "The children will come home from school soon. I have to be there."

Or you say, "I only do this job because I have to pay the rent and taxes, and I have to buy food—that's why I do it. Otherwise, I wouldn't do this work." So you do things which you don't want to do. That's why you are unhappy and experience stress all the time. The cause of this stress is that you don't want to do your duties, yet you are forced to do them. And so, when you do them you resent them. It is your attitude that you have to change. You need to learn to do your duties with a spirit of love and joy. If you feel that you are acting under the pressure of your duties all day, then your duties make you a slave.

There are several points to remember: First, you cannot live without doing actions; second, you always receive the fruits of actions; third, you cannot live without doing your duties, and fourth, the wrong attitude toward your duties makes you a slave. So how can you be free? There is one important skill that you need to learn to be free: learn to love your duties.

Every time you think that you want to do something but you cannot, it creates pressure within you because you do not yet know how to love your duties. You feel that your duties are forced on you, and you do not know how to create love for them. You do your duties as a mere chore, and it is that which creates problems for you and makes you a slave. What you need to learn is to create love for your duties.

But what kind of love is that? You can learn to love by understanding one concept, and that is ahimsa. In the *Yoga Sutra* there are ten commitments. They are not commandments, but if you are committed to this path and decide to practice them, they will help you a great deal. The first step to practice, before all the other teachings, is ahimsa, or non-harming. Before you can know truth you have to learn ahimsa, or how to love. Before you can lead a joyous life and live positively in the world, you have to learn love.

But you don't even know what love means! You think that love means giving someone a cup of tea and then receiving two in return. But love really means giving—giving without any condition, constantly giving selflessly—because whenever you are truly selfless, you'll enjoy life. When you are not selfless, then the expectation that motivates you to give will actually create problems for you. That is not love. The difference between lust and love is that love means selfless action; lust means that you have expectations.

So learn to "grease" your duties with love. Love is the one thing that can help keep you from being a slave to your duties. When you learn to grease and oil your duties with love, then life flows smoothly. If you serve your husband with love, and your husband serves you and the children with love, then there will be no problems in life. Your nervous system will not be agitated, and you won't do things that you resent. Instead, you'll be happy all the time.

If you really want to help yourself, you need to understand the difference between habits and samskaras. Your habits have made your personality. They make a mask for you, and that is your outer shell, your external life. Samskaras are the accumulation of impressions stored in the unconscious mind that motivate you to do something again and again. Whatever you do, hear, or see leaves an impression in the unconscious mind, where there are many layers and levels of samskaras. They are the impressions of your actions and desires, asleep. Every now and then these samskaras become active, and then they motivate and control your mind and your emotions. For example, perhaps one day you feel very happy and you think, "I feel great! I have no anxieties," and then a samskara bubble arises in your mind and you suddenly become miserable. You do not have control over your samskaras, but they control your emotions, your inner life.

Students of yoga often talk about samskaras but don't really understand this term and simply use the concept to excuse their personal problems. For example, if I ask someone, "Why did you divorce your wife?" that person may reply, "It's my samskaras." Or they may have an accident, or a disease, or any problem and say that it's just due to their samskaras. But saying this does not help you because you don't know what you really mean, and you don't accept the responsibility for understanding yourself.

You know how to culture and cultivate only a small part of the mind—the conscious mind. But the conscious mind is actually controlled by the unconscious mind, and that is why it is not easy to make spiritual progress. The conscious mind functions through the senses, and whenever an event takes place that relates to an impression already in your mind, then that impression, or samskara, becomes active. And because all your actions leave some impression on your unconscious mind, those impressions become your samskaras. Thus, your samskaras control your life. So to make progress, your samskaras need to be purified.

But first, you must transcend your desires. There are only two known ways to do this: renounce your desires or fulfill your desires. You can do this by either renouncing your desires and then reducing them to a minimum, or by understanding which desires you want to fulfill and then by doing your duties. When you fulfill your desires by doing actions, however, you must remember that to do so, you must do your actions with love.

Renunciates and swamis purify their samskaras by offering them to the light, to that great fire within—burning them in the fire of knowledge. (Swamis wear saffron-colored garb to symbolize the color of fire, the color of knowledge. When they have the determination to say, "I have burned all my desires in the fire of knowledge," then they will wear that color.) They consciously bring forward all the latent, buried impressions during meditation, telling their mind that they are ready to face them, and if they have built that kind of determination and willpower, they can allow those samskaras to be burned mentally. They are all mental impressions; there is nothing solid or material here. All these past impressions can be burned, and then they are free of them. The goal is to expand the conscious aspect of the mind so that there is no unconscious. But this path is not for everyone.

There is another way to purify your samskaras: After you have transcended your desires, you can sit in deep meditation, build your determination, and tell your mind and your samskaras, "At this time, my mind is only for meditation. I have to meditate and learn to go beyond the mire of illusion and confusion created by my mind." Then you allow all the impressions to come forward and you don't get involved in them. That method is called "inspection within," or introspection, and slowly you learn to become a witness and transcend the samskaras.

If you always remember two things you'll never be sorry. These two things are death and the one reality. Death will help you realize that you eventually have to leave here, that this world is only a platform, and you are merely on a journey.

Remembering the reality will help you realize that you are strong. It is within you. Wherever you are walking, you are walking with that reality. Death is there to remind you that this physical self will finally go away, and not to become attached to the world. You have only to complete your duties and your responsibilities with love.

Chapter 9

SPIRITUALITY IN LOVING
RELATIONSHIPS

I don't understand how you can live without loving people. If you cannot love one person, how can you love the whole universe? And if you cannot love the universe, then what is the use of talking about divinity? The important part of your behavior is how loving you are.

This word "love" is the least understood and most misused of all words in the modern world. People tell their partners they love them, but often they don't really mean it. If they say, "I love you," they are lying to the other person. If you love someone you don't lie to them—that's not love! But many people know only one kind of language, and that is wounding someone's heart and mind by suggesting to them in person that they love them, and then when they're gone, resenting them and criticizing them to others.

Another serious problem is that people think that in order to love one person they have to exclude others. In the name of love, they become possessive, and then they hate or fear others. This insecurity develops, increases, and makes them miserable in their day-to-day life—and eventually it destroys them. That is why they cannot enjoy life; they are insecure and possessive of those they claim to love.

What a human being really needs is to clearly understand life, so that life's purpose can be fulfilled and attained. And this can be done if you do not scatter your energy and distract yourself. If you gather your energy, light the fire within, and bathe in that fire, then life is good. But if you scatter your energy, then your purpose in life will never be attained. So learn to enjoy life as it is. Every second of life should be enjoyed! The enjoyment of the past is gone, and the enjoyment in the future is only an imagination, so learn to enjoy life here and now. You need to understand how to tread the path of life and how to enjoy this procession of life without harming or hurting anyone.

According to yoga psychology, there are three qualities in human beings: the spiritual, the human, and the animal, or *sattva*, *rajas*, and *tamas*. The quality that establishes balance, tranquility, and equanimity in life is the *sattvic* quality. When you are sattvic and at peace you are serene and love all; you don't hate or feel jealousy for anyone. This is why yoga science teaches *ahimsa*, nonviolence. But if you want to practice non-violence, you must first know that love comes before truth; *satya* (truth) is developed later on, but first you have to understand ahimsa (love). You cannot practice truth if you do not understand ahimsa. Your goal is to practice love and to learn to speak the truth. The great bibles and scriptures of all the cultures in the world say you should love others and speak the truth. Your parents told you to do this, but their teachings didn't explain how. You need to have an example. Yoga science teaches that.

In developing love, the field of your practice is where you live—with your family, friends, colleagues, or neighbors. If you want to develop love, then you should do no violence. Whether you are learning to love your husband, wife, children, or friends, the first thing is to do no violence in action, speech, or mind. If you refrain from hurting, injuring, or killing, then you will naturally come to love. By observing this principle of ahimsa, you become loving, and then you can practice truth.

But your ego is a fortress that does not allow you to expand your personality and consciousness. The role of the ego should be to help you to function well in the external world, to coordinate your various activities in life, and to give direction to your mind's internal states. If you allow the ego to become dominant, then you cannot grow or attain anything of value either spiritually or personally.

There is a way to tell how much love you have for others: sit down quietly and calmly examine your fears. The more fear you have, the less love you have. If you have less fear, then you will have more love. If you have no fear, you are able to give complete love. Your fear will tell you how much love you are capable of. So learn to live in love and not in fear. Always be cheerful, compassionate, and giving. Let Providence work, and trust that you will receive what you need.

But in your observation and awareness in life, you normally concentrate on the externals rather than on your own personality. And unfortunately, the first thing that you usually learn is to watch others—you watch and judge how others move, talk, and feel—but you don't try to understand how or why you think, move, or speak. As a result, your entire energy becomes focused externally. All your attention becomes directed outside you, and then you do not work to eliminate your own negative habits. If you do not know yourself, you can never know or understand others. So if you want to learn about change or self-transformation, or if you want to understand how to make corrections in yourself, don't begin by trying to observe or correct others. In the external world everything is subject to movement: everything is fleeting and nothing is permanent. You have to live in such a world, and to do that well you have to understand yourself.

Love is learning to maintain respect for others. Love is not that spontaneous thing you feel for someone that is merely sensual. That feeling is not love; it dies in only a few days' time. Love is understanding; it is giving. When you love, you give and give and don't expect anything in return. And when you learn to give, when you understand that the real law of life is giving, and that the more you give, the more you receive, then you will know that love is giving sincerely, not expecting things from the other person all the time. Your expectations are the mother of all your problems in life: you expect too much from each other; you fantasize about relationships and expect too much of them—and you are then disappointed. Once you realize this, you can adjust your expectations and create harmony in the relationship.

Those who cannot love are actually selfish. But the more selfless you become, the more you will find that you have a kind of freedom that cannot be imagined by your mere mind. In the modern world you learn to live only for yourself, and you learn to value the things that you have or want to acquire for yourself. This is one approach to living. But if you understand that you are meant for others, and if you want to serve others and live for others, that is an entirely different way of living. The first way contracts your personality; the other expands your personality—that is the difference. So far, you've formed the habit of being selfish, and you see only your own viewpoint and desires.

All the great people of the different traditions in the world have been selfless. Christ, the Buddha, and Krishna all attained the highest wisdom because they were selfless—but still they remained themselves. Selfishness is not needed; it will get in your way. If you are selfless, your outer individual shell will remain exactly the same, but your inner light will expand to universal consciousness. That individual flame of love will become a conflagration that will burn up the weed of your selfishness. Truth will automatically come to you if you learn how to love.

But don't approach love in a merely external or superficial way; offering your body to somebody is not love; it is merely lust. I am talking of that kind of love in which you are completely selfless. In such love you want to give, and you feel great joy in giving, and you feel that this is something great for you to do as a human being. You need to learn to give and truly love.

The day you understand that you have not come to this world merely to fulfill your own selfish desires, that will be a great day for you. The word "service" in Sanskrit is *seva*, which also means "to enjoy." To serve others is not a process of merely helping others; you should actually enjoy the act. And the finest of all acts is to give without any strings or attachments. If you give sincerely and lovingly and then observe the results, you will realize that the best deeds you have done are those in which you gave without strings or attachments. The mother is a symbol of that kind of love because of the way she experiences a pain like death when she gives birth to her child. A mother does that out of love. She can deny herself anything; a good mother does everything for her child.

The *Bhagavad Gita* says, "The person of attainment, the enlightened person—how does he walk, how does he sit, how does he think?" Human beings can be understood and known by their behavior, actions, and speech. And those who have coordinated their thinking, speech, and actions harmoniously are truly beautiful. Good thoughts are those which are not negative, passive, or selfish. Good action is that which is meant to help others selflessly. You do not benefit personally from good actions, but you spontaneously do the right action to help others. That is the real concept of beauty. Real beauty lies in these three things: your actions, thoughts, and speech. So how do you allow your good thoughts to be brought into action? Prayer can help you, but prayer alone is not the answer to learning to work with your actions. You have to deal with them yourself, for you are the owner and master of those actions. Prayer helps in other ways, but not in the area of your actions.

You would like to be good but you cannot, because you have not been taught how. You don't understand the real value of life. You don't understand that the principle of life is giving. That is the only way to liberation. There is no other way. You can pray for a hundred years, become a great swami, and prosper, but if you do not understand that the principle of life is giving, you are doomed.

You do certain actions and then you think that you are a great karma yogi: you earn and become a good provider, or you feed your children and look after your wife, and then you think you are a great, spiritually advanced person. That's not enough. You should learn to do your duty with love. That is something great and profound. When you do your duties with real love, then that is loving action.

But you wonder how you know what your duties are. Whatever you do and wherever you are, pay attention to the things that are occurring in the present—that is your duty! Whatever comes in front of you is your duty. But if you do your duties mechanically, then you are no more advanced than the clock Big Ben, giving time to the world but not knowing that it is a timegiver. You should do your actions, but do them lovingly. Learn to create this attitude in your mind. If you do something for your wife, such as getting her a cup of tea or a glass of water when she's not well, then bring it to her with love. If you just bring water and slam it on the table, then you are doing the action, but it is not loving duty. All your actions should be greased with love.

The highest of all human creations is love, and you can

learn to create such love. Love does not drop suddenly from the heavens above. Love is consideration, caring, sharing, surrendering, and giving. Love itself means giving. Whoever you love, decide one important thing: that you will not hurt that person through your mind, action, or speech. Ahimsa (nonviolence) is the expression of love; they are one and the same. Learn to express love; learn to cultivate that attitude toward others.

At home all married people should learn to give to each other without any conditions or limitations. Outside the home, protect yourself first, and then act. But at home, you should rely totally on your partner and not protect yourself; act spontaneously. Great and gentle people who are wise will never allow their family life to be disturbed. Don't allow anyone to disturb your family life because your family is meant to be a temple of peace. When you are tired you can rush home to your wife and children and find solace there.

Many people believe that to walk the path of spirituality, they must leave their homes and families or go away to some other place. This is not helpful or necessary. The difference between the paths of renunciates and householders is that renunciates have plenty of time for practices, since they live on the charity of others, while householders have material means, but feel they have no time for spiritual practices. As householders, they are lost and distracted by earning a living, while renunciates are lost in brooding with their time. Householders think, "Oh, how well these priests, sages, swamis, and yogis live. They are the happiest people on the earth," but the yogis are thinking, "What are we going to eat tomorrow? We don't have anything!" If you want to progress on the spiritual path, stay where you are and learn the art of living and being with your family.

The purpose of a good life is to attain your natural needs conveniently, and then you can more easily explore the higher stages of life. But if you have many obstacles and difficulties, it is hard to explore the higher steps. All the things in the external world—making a good income, having a good home, and owning things that are helpful to you—are all means for attaining your natural needs. But the same things that can become the means to a higher goal can also create obstacles for you. In the family, a good husband or wife who helps you and shares with you is a means for your comfortable living, but this relationship can also create serious problems. Your problem is not with the means of the world, it is with the way you use them.

You have so little time in life, and you waste so much of it. You have to be constantly vigilant to utilize your time well, so that life becomes fruitful and useful, like a flower that blooms and gives its fragrance to all. The spiritual concept of marriage and home is that you should make that home and marriage a happy one so that it radiates your happiness to others. To help you accomplish this, the family institution is wonderful. Our home is meant for our inner spiritual experiments. Our home is our laboratory, and when we learn something about love in our home, then we can go out and do useful things in the community and the world. But if we fail at home, then we really fail.

Men and women are essentially two different forces. Both can attain enlightenment, but they have not yet learned how to genuinely love each other. This is a serious problem, and it is causing society to crumble and is hurting the future generation—your children—who you expect to be good citizens.

Consider who you are. You have a personality, and your personality is controlled by your particular and unique character. Over the course of your life and growth, your character has been woven by your habit patterns. You have a particular habit, and your spouse has a different type of habit, and so you decide that you are not compatible. You are both good people but your habit patterns feed your individual egos, and then you create a division or barrier between yourself and others, and you remain inside that ego boundary. The same thing happens to your spouse. You are both wonderful people, but you are not compatible because your habit patterns are different and conflicting.

Men and women expect the same thing: that the person of their dreams will come into their life one day, marry them, and make them happy—then their life's purpose will be fulfilled. They don't really understand why they want to get married. They say that they want to help the other person, but that's not really being honest. From the very beginning, the real purpose of marriage is not understood by either person, and thus they do not know how to make the marriage successful. They are disappointed because they are not realistic about marriage. You have to see life and marriage from a realistic viewpoint.

You want to get married because you are insecure; you cannot live without somebody, and that is why you want to marry someone; it's a simple thing. You also want to get married to be fulfilled. Your light needs acknowledgement. But you should also acknowledge the light in someone else. You are light and he is light, and the light is only one. Then why is there a problem? The problem lies in understanding this, and thus you create a barrier between yourself and reality.

From a spiritual perspective, why do you want to marry someone? Marriage does not exist for the sake of sex alone, because to experience sex alone you could go to anyone. There is much more to it. Why do you really want to marry? What is that urge inside you that forces you to find someone and marry? It is that deep within, you actually want to share and to give—and that is called love. So if you really want to love your partner, you should not love or respect only your partner's body and skills. You should love your partner because you see the divine shining through that face. There is a light in that lamp. You love the light. You don't love the wick, the oil, or the stand. You love the lamp for the sake of the light. You should establish the same awareness when you get married and establish a home—love the light in your partner. If you do not establish this awareness, it is because you are selfish.

There are two basic principles in life: the "law of contraction" and the "law of expansion." You need to understand how these principles apply to the spiritual path and to your goals in your family life. You say you want to expand your personality and consciousness, but you actually follow the principle of contraction in your attitudes and behavior. You think of yourself only as an individual, so you contract your personality and become increasingly selfish. When you follow the law of expansion, however, you learn that you are one with the universe. That realization should be your goal. If you remain only an isolated individual to the last breath of your life, then you have not grown—you have simply wasted your time and your life. The joy that we are meant to derive on all levels remains only on the selfish level, and you do not ever fully understand the purpose of life, and how relationships help you to expand your personality.

Sometimes men and women think that in marriage they will become one with their partner, but that's not possible. Don't try to do that; for two to become one in that way is not possible. Instead, you should become like an eleven—two separate and independent numbers. If two people consider themselves to be like an eleven, then they will enjoy this life together because each is respected as an individual—and as an individual you respect the other person's independence. If you have this attitude to begin with, try to understand the other person even more fully, and then add respect and love to that.

Marriage is a truly great experience, an institution that

should be adored and understood. It is meant to be a center of love that radiates, but, unfortunately, in the modern world, that marriage center has most often become a center of hatred. Both men and women express their resentment and anger at their partner; they feel that there's nothing else they can do—what's done is done. With that kind of attitude they live together under the same roof, nagging and being nagged their whole life. They criticize each other and waste their time and energy analyzing each other's faults, and all their energy in this relationship is wasted. There is no reason for people to live like that. It would be better for them to establish under-standing and a bridge between each other. When you realize that you have committed a mistake, simply do not repeat it— and then you are free; you are forgiven by yourself. And if you have forgiven yourself, then the Lord has forgiven you. Usually, however, you have guilt feelings because you haven't forgiven yourself, and when you don't forgive yourself, then you project your anger and negative feelings onto others and make their life miserable.

Often your love does not grow and develop because it does not come from a state of understanding. Love means first understanding each other, and then accepting each other as you are. If you really love someone it's not that difficult to adjust to each other when you decide to marry. But it is better not to marry than to get married and then become divorced— to hurt someone or to be hurt by someone.

I have observed marriages throughout the world, and I have learned that arranged marriages have often been more successful than these modern so-called "love marriages," when you show only your best parts to the other. This sort of love does not lead you anywhere; it's based only on superficiality. But marriage is something powerful, sacred, and wise. If you accept someone, and if you are accepted by someone, you should learn to understand that person, adjust to them, and give to them selflessly. Don't try to destroy someone's personality. Learn to understand, adjust, and give unconditionally. A relationship becomes easy if you understand each other and accept each other as you are— then you can help each other. But in America I've observed that if a wife and husband fight, they don't try to repair the relationship; they just look for a replacement. There is no such thing as repair; there is only replacement!

In your daily life you need to remember that contentment is your goal. And if you want to be happy and content, you need to learn how to adjust and adapt within yourself and to others. You need to adjust your mind, actions, and speech so that they are compatible with others whose mind, action, and speech do not relate exactly to yours. You'll find that you have problems doing this, but at the same time, if you follow this process, you'll also find that you become free and contented. If you want to be content and happy without understanding how to adjust, that will never happen.

I once lectured at a conference in Germany that five hundred prominent psychologists attended. They invited me to speak, so I said, "If you allow me to say the truth, I will come." I asked the audience how many of them were divorced, and most of them were. So I told them that they were responsible for the crumbling and disintegration of society. I wanted to confront them: if counselors believe that divorce is better than learning to adjust to each other, then how can they help people remain married?

Sometimes the partners think that psychologists are modern gurus, so whatever they say must be right, but sometimes these counselors don't really try to understand and help the couple. People pay counselors to help them improve their marriage, but the therapists tell them to separate, and the patients don't know that these counselors are only projecting their own inner feelings and conflicts onto the process.

If two people come with great hope and pay money to receive help, and the therapist says they should separate for some time and see how they feel, that's not a cure for the problem. Therapists should not make a living by encouraging such things; they should learn to create bridges and better understanding between partners. Where couples are not communicating, they should try to help them to communicate more effectively. If the therapist does this, then counseling is a good and helpful profession.

Teachers, doctors, psychologists, and counselors should try to counsel and assist their patients so that misunderstandings are eliminated. They should teach people to understand each other, and reestablish communication so that family life is not destroyed. Otherwise, the children suffer most.

Why does one couple live together happily when another couple does not, although they are all good people? Many couples lead successful, prosperous, and busy lives but do not know how to have a close dialogue with their partner, and do not discuss things or communicate fully. For them, many important things in life remain unspoken and are not understood. They do not learn to expand their personality and communicate. If you think, "I wish my husband loved me," or, "I wonder if my wife loves me; she never expresses it to me," you may get divorced because the love is not expressed, even though both people are wonderful. You do not know how to really express your love, but you seek love your whole life. There is no animal or creature who does not crave love. But what is that love which you crave? What do you mean by love, and how can you find it? If I ask you to describe what you seek, you will fail: you cannot describe love itself. Whenever you try to describe it, you end up describing actions because you cannot explain what love itself is.

The most ancient language in the world is the language of

love. Sometimes you can express your love through your feelings alone, without any speech or action. For example, when you are in love you use a peculiar language, and you may make gestures which are not normal in other situations, but they are accepted by those you love. You may tease someone or make a funny face if you are in love with someone, and the other person will like it; but if you did that publicly with another person, they would be offended. This language doesn't lie or misinform or distort the world, unlike the language we use for manners or politeness. That language is only empty words which have no heart or love.

People fight because they don't understand each other. So learn to discuss things with your partner; all problems can be solved and resolved if you discuss them. And when you discuss things, don't be stubborn or domineering, with the attitude that because the person is your wife or husband, they have to listen to you. Don't forget that you are the two separate and individual lines of the eleven. There should be a sense of equality between you.

But weak moments come in everyone's life when there is a gap in communication. And when you do not communicate with your own husband or wife, it means the problem lies with you and not with the other. Both partners should think that way. They should learn to discuss things. Never leave things undiscussed; then your communication is broken.

In all situations, learn to discuss things and to communicate. Sometimes it doesn't matter if you even call your partner names; this is letting out your feelings, and it can sometimes be therapeutic if it does not go beyond that. You should also allow others to let out their anger or frustration, and you should learn to receive it. You should have the understanding that when the other person is angry you will not speak or argue. Then you will really understand each other. If you allow the other person to let out his anger, then after a few minutes he will say, "I'm sorry," and you can resolve the problem. Learn to have patience with each other.

Communication does not begin on the physical level or through speech or letters. Real communication starts on the thought level, long before you express yourself in letters or words. You and I have been communicating long before you even thought of reading this book or I thought of writing or lecturing. Communication between two people starts even without their knowing it, without their even seeing each other. Communication originates from the thinking level, and then you express yourself externally, through your speech or actions. So learn to express your feelings and thoughts to your partner. Learn to understand each other; make your life beautiful. Time is short, the work is vast, and we have to cross this mire of delusion. It cannot be done by being all alone.

One of the great Persian poets said, "On the ladder of love, the first rung is reverence." The moment you lose respect for your partner, there is something wrong with you. The moment you feel a lack of respect for your wife or husband, your love is gone. The word *bhakti* means "love plus reverence"—to have both reverence and love for the other person. So learn to give with reverence, and then there will be no conflict between you. Respect does not just "go away"; if it is gone, try to establish it again and again. If misunderstandings rob the purity of your reverence from your heart and mind, then work to reestablish it.

Once I met a couple, and the woman was as beautiful as a statue, but her husband loved someone else. The man respected his wife, but he did not love her. I wondered how the other woman could be superior to such a beautiful woman, so I said to the husband, "Your wife is most beautiful! Everyone in the whole country thinks you have the most beautiful wife!" and he suddenly began to cry. I asked, "Does she love you?"

He said, "I don't think so, but my girlfriend does."

Happiness in married life has nothing to do with the attractiveness of faces, dresses, or such things. These last for only a few days, months, or years. The best part of a human being, that which is really important and beautiful, that which can be enjoyed most, is their behavior—the way they talk, walk, act, and gesture—that is real beauty.

Human relationships could be truly joyous; they could create a great and complete happiness if two human beings really understood and accepted each other, and learned how to follow the spiritual path together. All the great religions repeat one message: God is the principle of equality, love, peace, and happiness—within and without—which is omnipresent, omniscient, and omnipotent. If that is true, then who are you and from where did you come? You have come from that love and peace. You live in it. So that love, peace, and happiness are within you, too.

When you go to the source within and see that light in your partner, then you realize, "My partner is not a mere body or an object of sensory gratification, but a human being who has that light of divinity within." When both partners realize that, then your relationship is a temple. And when you understand that a human being is a shrine, then you don't need to go to an external temple, church, or chapel to pray. That experience is love: love means knowing the truth within. Then, suddenly, you will discover yourself giving all that you have without any condition—because you have understood the truth. Without love, there is no meaning in anything.

If there is ever a profound and peaceful "revolution" in the world, it will take place within the family. When human beings fully understand life, they will not create revolution in the streets, damaging and destroying things in the external world. The real revolution will begin in the home. So how do we create a good home? How do we have healthy children? How do we create the kind of discipline that is healthy for children? Once we know how to do this we can change the whole world: we can take another step in the development of civilization. We have done enough research on mind, matter, and energy. We know that if we decide today that we really want a good and healthy society, and if we decide we want to change our society, we can change it in thirty or forty years. But to do that we will have to change ourselves and our habits so that we have healthy children, and so that the children learn from the very beginning to love and to share. It is possible to achieve this.

Family life is the ground for training children. When you are a child, your mother and father should teach you to walk and move in a straight, comfortable, and balanced way. They should teach you to speak in a balanced and pleasant way, and to interact pleasantly with others. And when you have learned those basic things, then *acharyas* (teachers) explain to you the "why" of life; they answer the questions: Why are we alive? How should we live?

But if the parents have not done their work, it becomes very hard for students to change and develop. The teacher tells them to come to him, but they go in the opposite direction because they have already become resistant, stubborn, and negative. They don't accept things as they are. They accept things only if they are as they want them to be. That is a serious problem in their learning. To learn to "let go" is an important part of childhood training. Those who are fortunate have received that training.

It is the adults who hurt the children: the children are beautiful and wonderful, but their parents do not consider the effect of their own selfishness on the children's welfare. Parents feel that a child is theirs, and that the child should do what they want. Such pressure, domination, and suggestions from others do not allow children to grow naturally.

When you become selfish, you create boundaries around

yourself; you live in an imaginary self-created fortress. When you become selfless, then you expand your personality because you are not thinking of yourself alone. Many people do not communicate well with others or trust others because they were not taught to give. And that is why a great teacher once said, "Give me the first seven years of a child's life, and the rest you can have." The best and most important period of life is childhood, and if the right seeds are sown then one truly grows and develops.

But in the modern world our responsibilities as human beings are not usually imparted in childhood, and that is why people remain irresponsible and selfish throughout life. The first teacher is not the one who teaches children philosophy or yoga; it is actually the mother. And if the mother was a bad teacher, then the grown children always have a cross to bear in life, or an obstacle to overcome in their growth—and throughout their life they don't trust anyone.

Children learn through imitation and example; they don't learn through books, mere words, or through culture or philosophy. They learn by seeing what others do. So to use and benefit from family life, you should learn the universal principle, the law of karma: "As you sow, so shall you reap." Whatever actions you undertake always have consequences— some helpful and some unhelpful.

Children do not need just simple, tender care. What is important is behavior, and right behavior is learned by children in the home when parents behave well and teach their children to communicate positively with others. Children learn by example, so if the parents do not set a good example, then the children will grow up with problems in how they relate to others. If you behave badly toward your partner, you are not only harming your partner, you are also harming your children, the future generation of the world, who, you expect, will convert it into a Garden of Eden.

This is the problem: you expect your children to learn what you say, but they actually learn what you do. You always want the best for your children; you don't want them to pick up your bad habits. You know what your bad habits are: what is bad in you is what is unhealthy in you. You may not want to admit this to yourself, but you know it. Your bad habits are your arrogance, your egotism, your selfishness. Actually, all these traits can be summed up in one word—selfishness.

For example, when a child sees his parents lie, the child misbehaves or lies. The father or mother gets angry and spanks the child, so the child is bewildered. "My mother and father lie," they think, "so why am I not supposed to lie?" On the other hand, when a mother and father are good examples for the child, then that child is happy and secure and grows up without fears or selfishness. But modern society is still in a primitive state; it has not yet attained the height of a culture in which you learn to truly give to your children. So these days, although human beings are growing, it happens in a wild and selfish way.

And here is another thing. While you are learning to teach your children, you should want to learn from your children, too. Just as parents are teachers for their children, children are also teachers for their parents. But often parents don't have the intense desire to learn that children have. You should learn to keep that zeal alive in yourself. Never close the gates of learning; they should remain open. Don't allow yourself to think that you know everything. Always remember that you still have more to learn. There is no end to your learning.

First, children learn through imitation and example. Then, when the time is right, the next step comes: They begin to learn from the way those around them behave and feel. They develop empathy. Then, if someone cries, their heart also cries. They could become cruel, however, and hate that person if they had not developed empathy. But that is not the natural response. If children grow up in an atmosphere that is not healthy, how do you expect them to become good citizens, and to help others? So parents should carefully observe how their children's personality is growing and developing. They should be attentive and careful to impart the subtle lessons that help children grow. If children are trained correctly, then they will learn to give. Those who want to have children, and those who are already parents, should learn to give up their selfishness and give their children the kind of knowledge that is helpful and healthy for them so that they can, in turn, impart the same knowledge to their own children. That kind of sacrifice is higher and more difficult than the mere idea of giving.

You should create in your children the zeal and desire to learn to give, and to instill that, you should have compassion. Compassion means that you love your children, and you want your children to grow, learn, understand, and practice. But before anything else, you have to prepare your children to learn. This is more important than imparting your teaching. When you learn how to prepare your children, you teach them basic things. If a solid foundation is not there, then a castle cannot be built. If a castle is built on sand without the right foundation, it cannot stand. The foundation is primary, and the cornerstone of that foundation is your compassion.

Sometimes wisdom flows through you. When you have compassion, all good things will come through you, but if you don't have compassion, and if you are selfish, then only the negative will come out of you. When you are learning to teach your children, your first responsibility is to develop compassion for them. You can do wonders with the help of compassion. If it is not there, then imparting knowledge is like planting seeds in a barren field in which nothing will grow.

So I encourage parents to practice ahimsa (love). This requires strength; love is inner strength. Love alone is the only real strength. The sages live in the forest and they have no weapons to protect them, but they remain safe because they practice nonviolence to such a degree that even the most violent animal becomes calm in their presence.

I had that experience once near Rishikesh, where there is a temple called Chandakali, in a deep forest. There was a swami who lived there in a thatched hut, and the whole forest around it was full of tigers.

One night I went to see the swami at eleven o'clock, and he said, "How did you come here all alone? It is very dangerous to travel at this hour. You should go back now!"

I exclaimed, "You just said that it is dangerous to travel now, but you are sending me back into danger again!"

So he half-heartedly allowed me to remain and sit down. He was baking a large bread in a *dhuni*, a kind of fire, and the loaf was rising and swelling. I asked, "What is this huge bread? It is big enough to feed twenty people!"

He said quietly, "My kids eat a lot."

I was surprised and asked him where his kids were, and if he was married, and he answered, "Yes." But there was no cottage around.

Suddenly I heard a roar—tigers! The swami said to me, "One of my kids has come now," and the tiger came and sat down near him.

My whole body suddenly shivered and shook, and I thought, "I am finished now!"

The swami said to me, "Be quiet, please," and he broke the bread in half and asked the tiger, "What happened to the other kid?" And then the tiger's mate came and sat down near him and looked at him, and the swami gave them the two huge pieces of bread. Then he clapped his hands and said, "Go now," and the tigers left. He said, "I tamed them, you know. I live here alone. Sometimes I felt lonely so I started talking to the animals." It is possible to do that. I have even known of people who tamed wild elephants with love.

Your love should go beyond the boundaries of culture, religion, and country. It should include the entire universe. That's why the great sages say, "The whole universe is our home. We are all friends." The day that you learn to love all and exclude none, that is the day of your enlightenment. If you are waiting for enlightenment in your next life, then I have nothing to teach you. You can wait, but you'll be sorry. You'll come back and do the same thing over again. So do not postpone your enlightenment. You can attain it here and now. The first step is to learn to do your actions with love and learn to give. Then you'll know that every human being is responsible for making their life happy and then to emanate that happiness to others.

Spirituality alone can make you happy. The human frame will not make you happy. You and your partner are together to attain something and that is spirituality. Then you are fulfilled. Your first goal is to acknowledge the reality and the divine in your partner. If you cannot love one person, how can you claim to love others? How can you claim to love the universe or the cosmos? To begin the process, learn to be loving to your husband or wife and your children. Set aside a time to talk to each other. Let out your feelings in a creative way, and enjoy life. That is the path of spirituality in family life.

Chapter 10

THE PROCESS OF MEDITATION

Many students misunderstand meditation. They think it means withdrawing from the world and avoiding their responsibilities and relationships. Meditation is not needed for this; you already have many ways to avoid your duties. Meditation is the simple and exact process of becoming aware of who you are. It is the practice of gently freeing yourself from the worries that gnaw at you so that you can be free and respond to the needs of the moment and experience the joy of being fully present. Meditation is not what you think, for it is beyond thinking. You do not meditate on your problems in order to solve them, but through meditation you see through the problems you have set up for yourself. It is a definite process for resolving conflicts, and that can be learned when you understand yourself.

Your ancient teachers knew how to meditate, but you have forgotten. You have become dissipated; you have forgotten yourself in the rush of external stimuli. You've gone far away from yourself. Come home, or you will only succeed in creating a huge asylum in the world.

Meditation has nothing to do with beliefs. It is not allied to any religion or culture. It is a practical means for calming yourself, for letting go of your biases and seeing what is, openly and clearly. It is a way of training the mind so that you are not distracted and caught up in its endless churning. It teaches you to systematically explore your inner dimensions.

I teach only the methods which I have learned and which have been verified. If you can accept them for your spiritual health, growth, and well-being, that is good, for meditation is a system of commitment, not commandment. You are committing to yourself, to your path, and to the goal of knowing yourself. It is not a commandment from outside yourself.

Some Westerners are uncomfortable with the word "meditation." They forget that the Bible clearly says, "Be still and know that I am God." Learning how to be still is the method of meditation, and if you meditate regularly you will find that you have become more calm, yet more alert to what is needed at the time.

Most people associate calmness with passivity, but the peace that meditation brings releases energy. Worry and preoccupation dissipate your strength. Meditation frees the energy that has been bound in your mental conflict so that you can apply yourself one-pointedly to whatever you decide to do. Meditation will lead your mind to become more concentrated so that you can fully focus on whatever you choose. Because of this, those who meditate will learn almost anything more easily and more quickly.

From childhood onward you are taught to examine and understand things in the external world, but nobody teaches you to look within and understand the mind and its various states. All of your training has been to know the outer world, and to become skillful at manipulating it for your own benefit. But unless you learn to know yourself, whatever you do in the external world will not produce the results you want. If a tire is out of balance, no matter how wonderfully it was designed in other respects, no matter how much research went into compositing the material or designing the tread, it will not function properly. Unless you achieve inner balance, no matter how much you know about performing in the outer world, you will fall short. Meditation is the means of achieving this inner balance. Those who have examined the objects of the external world understand their transitory nature and know that life has more to give. Then they start searching within themselves, conducting "inner research."

Many students turn toward meditation out of curiosity or excitement, and try to understand themselves and know their internal states. But to do research in the interior world, we have to apply an exact science if we want to know the center of consciousness hidden deep in the inner recesses of our being. Some give up, but those who persist will find that meditation is a simple and exact procedure for becoming aware of who you really are. It is learning to know yourself.

If you don't want to know yourself, or don't care to know yourself, then no one can force you. But as you grow, you will come to a point at which you will want to know your deeper self, and then you become committed to the idea that you will know yourself on all levels in this lifetime.

The method of meditation is not a ritual belonging to any particular religion, culture, or group. All the great religions have come from one and the same reality, and without knowing this reality the purpose of life cannot be accomplished. There is a vast difference between prayer and meditation. Prayer is a petition from someone who has a particular desire to be fulfilled; meditation is a process that leads one from the gross self to the subtlemost self. But there is a good reason to pray, because when you pray you gain energy, courage, zeal, and strength from within. That is the real reason for prayer. Prayer definitely purifies the way of the soul. So do not disturb your practice of religion—but also learn to know yourself on all levels.

Meditation is a systematic technique. It is like a ladder with many rungs which finally leads to the roof, and from there one can see the vast horizon all around. Contemplation is another technique. It is different from meditation. It is also a systematic method for examining the principles of life and the universe. Through contemplation the aspirant constantly assimilates these ideas, and in time the whole personality is transformed. Those who are fully dedicated and have given their life to the goal of self-realization use both methods—meditation in deep silence and contemplation in daily life. Contemplation is seeking and searching for truth; and practicing meditation is experiencing truth. Those who are students of life can clearly understand the difference between prayer, meditation, and contemplation. They are different tools and different ways for attaining the goal of life. Though the schools of meditation and contemplation are two different schools, they can both help students to go beyond and establish themselves in their essential nature, which is peace, happiness, and bliss.

To become a good citizen, to become an evolved human being, to become a better follower of your own religion, or a better participant in your own culture, you have to meditate. All the great men and women of wisdom meditated. Christ certainly meditated. Moses, Rama, and Krishna were all people of meditation. Meditation establishes your conviction, and then your faith is strengthened. Then, your faith cannot be shattered or scattered by anything on the earth. This is the process of training yourself.

Meditation will give you a tranquil mind. Meditation will make you aware of the reality deep within. Meditation will make you fearless; meditation will make you calm; meditation will make you gentle; meditation will make you loving; meditation will give you freedom from fear; meditation will lead you to the state of inner joy called samadhi. These are the results of meditation. If you understand these goals and want to meditate, then it will help you, but if you are expecting to become rich through meditation, then don't do it.

Meditation is not a difficult task that you must force upon yourself; once you experience that inner joy you will spontaneously want to meditate as much as you now look forward to outer pleasures. Nevertheless, it is helpful to establish a routine to your meditative practice. Just as you eat at certain times of the day, and look forward to eating as those times approach, so too, by developing the habit of meditating at the same time each day, your whole being— body, breath, and mind—will look forward to meditating at that time. You should sit down every day at exactly the same time. Such training is powerful. If you want to learn to meditate, follow the process of establishing a specific time for your practice.

The first thing you have to learn is to be still. This begins with physical stillness. According to the tradition that we follow, the *asana*, or meditative posture, is carefully selected according to your nature and capacity, and you are guided by a competent teacher to keep your head, neck, and trunk straight. After choosing a sitting posture, good students learn to become accomplished in it.

After you have become still with the help of the meditative posture, you will become aware of obstacles arising from muscle twitching, tremors occurring in various parts of the body, shaking, and itching. These obstacles arise from lack of discipline, because we have been trained to move in the external world faster and faster, but the body has never been trained to be still. To learn this stillness, you should form a regular habit, and to form this habit you should learn to be regular and punctual, practicing the same posture at the same time and at the same place every day until the body stops rebelling against the discipline given to it. This step, though basic, is important and should not be ignored. Otherwise, you will not be able to reap the fruits of meditation, and your efforts will be wasted.

You should find a simple, uncluttered, quiet place where you will not be disturbed. Sit on the floor with a cushion under you or in a firm chair, with your back straight and your eyes closed. Then bring your awareness slowly down through your body, allowing all of the muscles to relax except those that are supporting your head, neck, and back. Take your time and enjoy the process of letting go of the tension in your body. Meditation is the art and science of letting go, and this letting go begins with the body and then progresses to thoughts.

Once the body is relaxed and at peace, bring your awareness to your breath. Notice which part of your lungs are being exercised as you breathe. If you are breathing primarily with your chest you will not be able to relax. Let your breathing come primarily through the movement of the diaphragm. Continue to observe your breath without trying to control it. At first the breath may be irregular, but gradually it will become smooth and even, without pauses and jerks. Continue to be aware of the breath.

Meditation is a process of giving your full attention to whatever object you have chosen. In this case you are choosing to be aware of the breath. Allow yourself to experience your breathing in an open and accepting way. Do not judge or attempt to control or change it. Open yourself so fully that eventually there is no distinction between you and the breathing. In this process many thoughts will arise in your mind: "Am I doing this right? When will this be over? My nostril is clogged—should I get up and blow my nose before I continue? Perhaps I should have closed the window. I forgot to make an important call. My neck hurts." Hundreds of thoughts may come before you, and each thought will call forth some further response: a judgment, an action, an interest in pursuing the thought further, an attempt to get rid of the thought.

At this point, if you simply remain aware of this process instead of reacting to the thought, you will become aware of how restless your mind is. It tosses and turns like you do on a night when you cannot fall asleep. But that is only a problem when you identify with the mind and react to the various thoughts it throws at you. If you do, you will be caught in a never-ending whirlwind of restless activity. But if you simply attend to those thoughts when they arise, without reacting, or if you react and attend to the reaction, then they cannot really disturb you. Remember—it is not the thoughts that disturb you, but your reaction to them. It is not a sound that disturbs your meditation, but your reaction to it.

Meditation is very simple. It is simply attending. You can begin by attending to your breath, and then if a thought comes, attend to it, notice it, be open to it—and it will pass. Then you can come back to the breath. Your normal response is to react to all your thoughts, and this keeps you ever busy in a sea of confusion. Meditation teaches you to attend to what is taking place within without reacting, and this makes all the difference. It brings you freedom from the mind and its meandering. And in this freedom you begin to experience who you really are, distinct from your mental turmoil. You experience inner joy and contentment, you experience relief and inner relaxation, and you find a respite from the tumult of your life. You have given yourself an inner vacation.

But this inner vacation is not a retreat from the world. It is only the foundation for finding inner peace. You must also learn to apply the principle of attending in your worldly activities so that you can apply yourself in the world more effectively. Through practicing meditation you can learn to be open to what comes before you in the world, giving it your full attention.

Ordinarily, you react to the experiences that come before you in the world in much the same way that you react to your thoughts. If someone says something negative to you, you become upset or depressed. If you lose something, you react emotionally. Your mood depends on what comes before you and, as a result, your life is like a roller coaster ride. You react before you have fully experienced what you are reacting to; what you see or hear immediately pushes a button. You interpret that according to your expectations, fears, prejudices, or resistances. You short-circuit the experience, and thus you limit yourself to one or two conditioned responses. You give up your ability to respond to a situation openly and creatively.

But if you apply the principle of meditation in that situation, you can fully attend to what is taking place. You can attend to your initial reaction without reacting to your reaction: "Oh, look at how threatened I feel by that." You need not deny your reaction. Let yourself be open to experiencing it, and it will move through you and allow other spontaneous responses to also come forward, so that you can select the one that is most helpful in that situation.

In this way meditation is therapeutic. It not only leads to inner balance and stability, it also exposes your inner complexes, your immaturities, your unproductive reflexes and habits. Instead of living in these and acting them out, they are brought to your awareness and you can give them your full attention. Only then will they be cleared.

This method of meditation is an inner method which has been thoroughly explored for centuries by the great sages. Just as scholars collect and examine the works of others, so also should meditators collect the teachings from various traditions and examine them before they apply a particular method that suits them. But don't do anything for your teacher's sake; do your practice for yourself.

Competent teachers instruct students in how to be free

from external influences and how to follow the primary steps so that the body, senses, and mind are prepared for meditative experiences. Students may have experiences on many levels, but not all experiences guide them. If the preliminaries are ignored, then students may waste years and years hallucinating and fantasizing, simply feeding their ego and not attaining any deeper experiences. A valid experience is the deep experience which can guide students. A valid experience is so clear that they do not need any external evidence to support it. Such an experience is gained only when students attain a state of equanimity and tranquility.

Doubts and fears may arise in their mind, but when students decide to tread the path of meditation, they sincerely prepare and discipline themselves. They examine all their "instruments" in the laboratory of life—body, senses, breath, and mind are attuned toward meditation alone.

And in the same way that students make a sincere effort to find a competent teacher and a suitable method of meditation, so also does a teacher search for good students who are fully prepared to take this voyage from the known to the unknown.

But there is one serious problem. Modern students are like children who plant seeds in the evening, and early the next morning wake up and start digging up the seeds to see what has happened. Of course nothing has happened; the seeds are still there so the child covers them up again and pours water on them. Then, in the afternoon, the child wants to examine the seeds again. Let the seeds of your practice grow; give your practice some time to develop.

You are frustrated for many reasons, and you place the blame on the meditation process. You should do your part, but often this is the problem: you are not fully playing your part. When the question of eating good-tasting food or another tempting distraction comes, you don't remember your meditation. At other times, when your meditation time comes and you cannot meditate, you blame the meditation itself. This is not fair; you must do things systematically. Every action has a reaction. It is not possible for you to do meditation and not receive benefits. You may not notice those benefits now, but slowly and gradually you are storing the samskaras (impressions) in the unconscious that will help you later. If you sow a seed today, you don't reap the fruit tomorrow, but eventually you will. It takes time to see results. Be gentle with yourself.

You sometimes expect to experience foolish things in meditation—you want to see lights and colors. If you meditate with such ideas, you will never really meditate. Meditation means gently fathoming all the levels of yourself, one after another. Be honest at least with yourself. Don't care what others say about their experiences—keep your mind focused on your goal. Shallow methods lead you only so far, but the systematic method of meditation can help you attain the highest of all states. You should not dive into shallow waters; the pearls of life are found in the deep ocean, not in ponds, lakes, or rivers.

It is your own mind that does not allow you to meditate, and an untrained mind is like a garbage disposal. To work with your mind, you'll have to be patient, you'll have to work gradually with yourself. The first step is concentration. Whatever you do—whether you are an accountant or a dancer—you have to be able to concentrate. If you are a musician, for example, and you can concentrate, then the more you concentrate, the more subtle your skills will become, and then the music develops and becomes very pleasing to yourself and to others. So the first step in meditation is concentration, and you can attain that depth of concentration if you train yourself.

But on what object or focus do you meditate? The mind always wants to have something to focus on or it flies away to some picture, object, or idea. If you do your meditation systematically, however, it is a complete process for training yourself. If you practice meditation systematically, even for only one month, it will help you. The important thing is that you should know how to work with yourself, how to know the inner self. You must do your practice. Otherwise the teacher cannot do anything. The teacher's responsibility is fifty percent; the other fifty percent is the student's. When you encounter obstacles, the teacher will help you, but if you don't do your part and you expect the teacher to do his, then there's nothing anyone can do. So learn to know yourself. Don't use the excuse that you don't have enough time—you have sufficient time to accomplish that.

You sometimes say, "I have not attained anything; I have been doing meditation for thirteen years!" Are you sure that you have been doing meditation? Or did you sit and sleep or dream or think? For thirteen years you have been thinking about many other things in the name of meditation; you think about your work and your boyfriend or girlfriend. You sat for all those years in meditation but you did not really meditate, and then you complain that nothing has happened to you. Do not give your mind space to wander when you meditate, but go step-by-step in the process. Train yourself. First, pay attention to your posture. Learn to sit correctly. Do your practice systematically. Then work to eliminate the mental and emotional obstacles. If meditators probe the inner levels of their being, exploring the unknown dimensions of interior life, and if they have learned a systematic and scientific method that can lead them to the next state of experience, then they can go beyond all the levels of their unconscious mind and establish themselves in their essential nature.

In the Bible, it is said that those who have an ear to hear will hear. When the mind becomes attuned, it is capable of hearing the voice of the unknown, and during deep meditation the ancient sages heard certain sounds called mantras. The sounds that are heard in such a state do not belong to any particular language, religion, or tradition. According to our tradition, which is a meditative tradition more than five thousand years old, mantra and meditation are inseparable, like the two sides of a coin. To do inner research, mantra and meditation are the greatest aids to a seeker. Mantra meditation is a concentrated, deep, and intense form of prayer, but it is not man-centered prayer; it is God-centered prayer.

All the existing spiritual traditions of the world use a syllable, a sound, a word or set of words, called a mantra, as a bridge for crossing the mire of delusion and reaching the other shore of life. *Mantra setu* is that practice which helps the meditator make the mind one-pointed and inward, and then finally leads to the center of consciousness, that deep recess of eternal silence where peace, happiness, and bliss reside.

There are those sounds that are created by the external world and heard by the ears, and there are those sounds heard in deep meditation by the sages. This sound is called *anahata nada*, the unstruck sound. Inner sounds do not vibrate in exactly the same way as sound vibrates in the external world. They have a leading quality. They lead the meditator toward the center of silence within. The following simile can help you understand this: Imagine that you are standing on the bank of a river and you hear the current as it flows. If you follow the river upstream, you will come to its origin. There, you will find that there is no sound. In the same way, a mantra leads the mind to the silence within. That state is called "soundless sound."

The mantra imparted by a teacher to a student is like a prescription given to a patient. There are innumerable sounds, each with a different effect. The teacher must understand which best suits a particular student, according to that student's attitudes, emotions, desires, and habits.

A mantra has four bodies or *koshas* (sheaths). First, as a word, it has a meaning; another more subtle form is its feeling; still more subtle is a presence, a deep intense and constant awareness of it; and the fourth, or most subtle level of the mantra, is soundless sound. Many students continue repeating or muttering their mantra throughout their entire life but never attain a state of *ajapa japa*, that state of constant awareness without any effort. These students strengthen their awareness, but meditate on the gross level only.

Those who go beyond this stage use special mantras that do not obstruct and disturb the flow of breath, but help regulate the breath and lead to a state called *sushumna awakening*, in which the breath flows through both nostrils equally. In this state the breath and mind function in complete harmony and create a joyous state of mind.

When students attain this state, the mind is voluntarily disconnected from the dissipation of the senses. Then they have to deal with the thoughts coming forward from the unconscious mind, that vast reservoir in which we have stored all the impressions of our lifetime. The mantra helps one to go beyond this process, creating a new groove in the mind, and the mind then begins to spontaneously flow into the groove created by the mantra. Finally, when the mind becomes concentrated, one-pointed, and inward, it peers into the latent part of the unconscious, and there, sooner or later, it finds a glittering light. The great ones like to keep their eyes partially closed, looking into the innermost light that shines within this frame of life. Mantra is the means. Meditation is the method.

My way of using the mantra is different from yours, however, because I do not want to fool around with the process. In my own practice I sit down and observe my whole being listening to the mantra. I do not remember the mantra or repeat the mantra mentally. Instead, I make my whole being an ear to hear the mantra, and the mantra is coming from everywhere. This will not happen to you immediately in meditation, but when you have attained or accomplished something, it will happen to you. Then, even if you do not want to do your mantra, it is not possible to avoid it. Even if you decide that you do not want to remember the mantra, it will not be possible. Finally, even the mantra does not exist; only the purpose for which you repeat the mantra is there; you are there. The mantra might still be there, but it exists as an experience that overwhelms your whole being, and is not separate from you.

The most important role mantra plays is during the transition period that every human being will experience. A dying person wants to communicate with his loved ones. The attachment that we create for mortal things and people produces serious and painful troubles for us at the time of death. Because we lack a clear philosophy which ought to have been developed during our lifetime, and because we have not practiced meditation and experienced the true self, our attachments become very painful. Death itself is not painful, but the fear of death is painful, especially for those who have not pondered the mystery of birth, death, and the hereafter. In such cases, these last moments of life cause extreme discomfort and even affect the voyage after death.

A dying person's senses do not function properly. They gradually lose the sense of sight, the tongue mumbles words that cannot be understood by others, and they are unable to express the mind's thoughts in speech or actions. But if they remember the mantra for a long time in such a state of loneliness, the mantra begins to lead them, and this miserable period is over when the mantra becomes their leader. Only one thought pattern is strengthened by remembering the mantra, and when it is firmly established it leads them to their abode of peace, happiness, and bliss.

The power of mantra and meditation can be validated if you quietly observe a sage, a rich man, or an intellectual on their deathbed. I have witnessed the joyful death of many sages. I have also witnessed the miserable death of rich men, scientists, and intellectuals. The agony in their facial expressions and their helplessness were proof to me that they had not prepared themselves for the last moment of life. So prayer, contemplation, and meditation should be taught, practiced, and experienced with full honesty, clarity of mind, and one-pointedness.

Never give up! Accept meditation as a part of your life, just as you eat, sleep, and do other things. Make it your goal to have a calm mind, to have a one-pointed mind, to have a tranquil mind. Do not give that up. The effect of your meditation reflects on your face. Meditation leaves a clear indication on your heart, and this is reflected on the face. When people speak to me, I can easily tell whether or not they meditate or are even capable of meditation. Their face is the index of their heart.

Those who live in the world can attain the highest state of samadhi through meditation. Then they are here, yet there; they live in the world, yet remain above; they include all, and exclude none. When the day arrives that every man, woman, and child practices meditation, we will all attain the next step of civilization and realize the unity in all. Liberation can be attained here and now, and that experience is the ultimate goal of human life.

GLOSSARY

ACHARYA • *A spiritual teacher or instructor. Literally, one whose character and behavior should be followed by others.*

AHAMKARA • *The sense of "I-am-ness." Literally, "the I-maker," or ego. The function of the mind through which pure spirit (purusha) falsely identifies with material and mental creation in the Sankhya and Yoga philosophies.*

AHIMSA • *Non-injuring, non-harming, or non-violence. The first of five moral restraints called yamas, which form the first step of the eightfold system of Raja Yoga.*

AJAPA JAPA • *That state of constant awareness of one's mantra without any effort.*

ANAHATA NADA • *Unstruck sound. Inner sounds which are heard in deep meditation by the sages and lead the meditator toward the center of silence within.*

ANTAHKARANA • *The "inner instrument" of the mind, consisting of: manas, or the active mind; buddhi, or the rational and intuitive intelligence; chitta, the mind-stuff and the reservoir of subtle impressions (samskaras); and ahamkara, the instrument of identification, the ego, or "I-maker."*

ASANA • *The meditative posture, carefully selected according to the nature and capacity of the student. A good student selects a sitting posture and learns to become accomplished in it.*

BHAKTI • *Love plus reverence; to have both reverence and love for the other person.*

BHIKSHA • *The act of begging or asking for alms.*

BRAHMAMUHURTA • *Three o'clock in the morning; an auspicious time for meditation.*

BUDDHI • *The powerful faculty of intellect. Buddhi is the faculty of mind that has three main functions: it knows, decides, and judges.*

CHITTA • *The pool of subconscious mind-stuff into which all the impressions gathered by the senses are thrown, as it were, and from the bottom of which they rise to create a constant stream of random thoughts and associations.*

DEVAS • *"Bright beings," or angels.*

DHUNI • *Kind of fire.*

KAMA • *The first of all the emotions; the prime desire. Kama is the mother of all other desires, and it gives rise to both the desire to satisfy or gratify the senses, and the beneficial desire to help others selflessly.*

KOSHA • *Body or sheath.*

KRODHA • *Anger.*

LOBHA • *Greed.*

MANAS • *The faculty which produces data for you from the external world. It is also the function which doubts and questions.*

MANTRA • *A sacred word with a profound meaning usually repeated and contemplated upon by meditators.*

MANTRA SETU • *The practice which helps the meditator make the mind one-pointed and inward, and then finally leads to the center of consciousness.*

MOHA • *Attachment; the sense: "This is mine."*

MUDA • *Pride.*

NIRODHA • *Control, not in the sense of suppression, but channeling or regulating.*

NIYAMAS • *The set of five personal commitments or observances. They are the second limb of the eightfold system of Raja Yoga as described in the Yoga Sutra of Patanjali. The niyamas attempt to cultivate positive habits which are conducive to self-realization. They are: purity of the body and mind (shaucha), contentment (santosha), practices to perfect the functioning of body, mind, and senses (tapas), self-study (svadhyaya), and surrender of the ego to the higher self (Ishvara-pranidhana).*

PRANA • *The life force. In the yogic tradition, prana is said to be tenfold, depending on its nature and function.*

PREYAS • *There are two categories of objects described in the Upanishads: shreyas and preyas. Preyas means that which is pleasant, and shreyas means that which is helpful.*

RAJAS • *One of the gunas (attributes of prakriti); activity. Rajas impels and energizes, overcoming stagnation.*

SAMADHI • *Spiritual absorption; the eighth rung of Raja Yoga. The tranquil state of mind in which fluctuations of the mind no longer arise.*

SAMSKARAS • *Subtle impressions of past actions.*

SANKALPA VIKALPA • *Constant doubt in the mind.*

SATSANGA • *Company of the sages; spiritual gatherings.*

SATTVA • *One of the gunas (attributes of prakriti). The sattva guna is characterized by purity, luminosity, lightness, harmony, and the production of pleasure. It is the purest aspect of the three gunas.*

SEVA • *Service; also means "to enjoy."*

SHADI • *Happiness, or marriage.*

SHREYAS • *There are two categories of objects described in the Upanishads: shreyas and preyas. Shreyas means that which is helpful, and preyas means that which is pleasant.*

SUSHUMNA • *The central channel through which kundalini energy is said to rise.*

TAMAS • *One of the gunas (attributes of prakriti). The tamas guna is characterized by solidity, stagnation, dullness, inertia, darkness, stasis, stupor.*

UPANISHADS • *The final portion of the Vedas, the ancient scriptures containing the wisdom of the sages. The philosophy of Vedanta is based on the Upanishads.*

VAIRAGYA • *Dispassion or non-attachment. According to the Bhagavad Gita, one does not necessarily need to renounce the world or what one needs, but one should perform their duties lovingly, skillfully, and selflessly, remaining unattached to the fruits of their actions.*

YAMAS • *The set of five restraints. They are the first limb of the eightfold system of Raja Yoga as described in the Yoga Sutra of Patanjali. The purpose of the yamas is to curtail behavior which is not conducive to spiritual growth. They are: nonviolence (ahimsa), non-lying (satya), non-stealing (asteya), control of passions, senses, and mind (brahmacharya), and non-attachment (aparigraha).*

ABOUT THE AUTHOR

One of the greatest adepts, teachers, writers, and humanitarians of the 20th century, Swami Rama is the founder of the Himalayan Institute. Born in Northern India, he was raised from early childhood by a Himalayan sage, Bengali Baba. Under the guidance of his master he traveled from monastery to monastery and studied with a variety of Himalayan saints and sages, including his grandmaster who was living in a remote region of Tibet. In addition to this intense spiritual training, Swami Rama received higher education in both India and Europe. From 1949 to 1952, he held the prestigious position of Shankaracharya of Karvirpitham in South India. Thereafter, he returned to his master to receive further training at his cave monastery, and finally in 1969, came to the United States where he founded the Himalayan Institute. His best known work, *Living with the Himalayan Masters*, reveals the many facets of this singular adept and demonstrates his embodiment of the living tradition of the East.

THE HIMALAYAN INSTITUTE

The main building of the Institute headquarters near Honesdale, Pennsylvania.

A leader in the field of yoga, meditation, spirituality, and holistic health, the Himalayan Institute was founded by Swami Rama of the Himalayas. The mission of the Himalayan Institute is Swami Rama's mission—to discover and embrace the sacred link, the spirit of human heritage that unites East and West, spirituality and science, and ancient wisdom and modern technology. Using timetested techniques of yoga, ayurveda, integrative medicine, principles of spirituality, and holistic health, the Institute has brought health, happiness, peace and prosperity to the lives of tens of thousands for more than a quarter of a century. At the Himalayan Institute you will learn techniques to develop a healthy body, a clear mind, and a joyful spirit, bringing a qualitative change within and without.

The Himalayan Institute's headquarters is located on a beautiful 400-acre campus in the rolling hills of the Pocono Mountains of northeastern Pennsylvania. In the spiritually vibrant atmosphere of the Institute you will meet students and seekers from all walks of life who are participating in programs in hatha yoga, meditation, stress reduction, ayurveda, nutrition, spirituality, and Eastern philosophy. Choose from weekend or weeklong seminars, monthlong self-transformation programs, longer residential programs, spiritual retreats, and custom-designed holistic health services, pancha karma, and rejuvenation programs. In the peaceful setting of the Institute, you will relax and discover the best of yourself. We invite you to join us in the ongoing process of personal growth and development.

Swami Rama transplanted his Himalayan cave to the Poconos in the form of the Himalayan Institute. The wisdom you will find at the Institute will direct you to the safe, secure, peaceful and joyful cave in your own heart.

"Knowledge of various paths leads you
to form your own conviction. The more
you know, the more you decide to learn."
—*Swami Rama*

PROGRAMS AND SERVICES INCLUDE:

- Weekend or extended seminars and workshops
- Meditation retreats and advanced meditation instruction
- Hatha yoga teachers' training
- Residential programs for self-development
- Holistic health services and pancha karma at the Institute's Center for Health and Healing
- Spiritual excursions
- Varcho Veda® herbal products
- Himalayan Institute Press
- *Yoga International* Magazine
- Sanskrit correspondence course

Living Joyfully magazine includes a quarterly guide to programs and is free within the USA. To request a copy, or for further information, call 800-822-4547 or 570-253-5551, write to Himalayan Institute, RR 1 Box 1127, Honesdale, PA 18431-9706 USA, or visit our website at www.HimalayanInstitute.org.

THE HIMALAYAN INSTITUTE PRESS

The Himalayan Institute Press has long been regarded as "The Resource for Holistic Living." We publish dozens of titles, as well as audio and video tapes, that offer practical methods for living harmoniously and achieving inner balance. Our approach addresses the whole person—body, mind, and spirit—integrating the latest scientific knowledge with ancient healing and self-development techniques.

As such, we offer a wide array of titles on physical and psychological health and well-being, spiritual growth through meditation and other yogic practices, and as well as translations of yogic scriptures.

Our yoga accessories include the Japa Kit for meditation practice, and the Neti™ Pot, the ideal tool for sinus and allergy sufferers. The Varcho Veda® line of quality herbal extracts is now available to enhance balanced health and well-being.

Subscriptions are available to a bimonthly magazine, *Yoga International*, which offers thought-provoking articles on all aspects of meditation and yoga, including yoga's sister science, Ayurveda.

For a free catalog call 800-822-4547 or 570-253-5551, e-mail hibooks@HimalayanInstitute.org, fax 570-647-1552, write to Himalayan Institute Press, 630 Main St., Ste. 350, Honesdale, PA 18431-1843, USA, or visit our website at www.HimalayanInstitute.org.